U-BOAT STORIES

U-BOAT STORIES

NARRATIVES OF GERMAN
U-BOAT SAILORS

EDITED BY
KARL NEUREUTHER AND CLAUS BERGEN

THIRTY-FOUR IN BLACK-AND-WHITE

AFTER DRAWINGS BY
CLAUS BERGEN

TRANSLATED BY
ERIC SUTTON

The Naval & Military Press Ltd

❖

Reproduced by kind permission of the Central Library,
Royal Military Academy, Sandhurst

Published by

The Naval & Military Press Ltd

Unit 10, Ridgewood Industrial Park,

Uckfield, East Sussex,

TN22 5QE England

Tel: +44 (0) 1825 749494

Fax: +44 (0) 1825 765701

www.naval–military–press.com

© The Naval & Military Press Ltd 2005

PREFACE

IT was with great pleasure that I accepted the invitation of the U-Boat Fellowship in Munich to edit and illustrate the experiences of the former U-Boat personnel who are members of this Association.

In the year 1917, when unlimited U-Boat warfare had been declared, I had the opportunity, for which I had long been anxious, of taking a long voyage in U 53, Captain-Lieutenant Rose, as an official painter. The memories that I carried away from that voyage have remained ineffaceable. Humanly speaking, the strongest impression that stayed with me was the spirit of fine and loyal comradeship, the iron bond that united officers and crew in the narrow space of the vessel, cut off, as they were, from home, far out upon an enemy-infested sea, completely self-dependent, beset by a hundred lurking perils and with death always before their eyes, offering their lives in chivalrous combat for the honour of their Fatherland.

One for all, and all for one ! Such was the supreme law of the U-Boat crews. Thus guided, they set forth, and they returned ; and many of the bravest lay united in death in their steel coffins on the ocean-bed.

Those who still live have kept faith with that ideal of comradeship ; and they have not forgotten their friend the painter. I hope that the experiences of a small U-Boat Association may testify to what iron will and fidelity can achieve against desperate odds, and in the extremity of peril.

That spirit of comradeship and faith is still alive. I hope that it may, in many distant places, sow a seed of conviction that unity and loyalty produce a strength that is invincible and leads surely to success.

In this sense :

Full speed ahead !

CLAUS BERGEN.

CONTENTS

C.   B.

U-BOAT STORIES

I

MY U-BOAT VOYAGE

By

Claus Bergen

" With the U-Boat flotilla at Heligoland you will certainly
have the best opportunity of seeing and painting whatever you
may choose. There you will see the various types of boats
ready for action in the harbour. You will have pleasant
quarters, and you might even find an opportunity of taking
part in a long voyage."

After a long and interesting employment as war painter on
the great modern ships of the line, one day I summoned up
courage, as I had long wished to do, to petition the Naval
Authorities for a transfer to the U-Boats. Not long afterwards
I found myself once more standing in the presence of that
energetic, forceful, unforgettable personality, the Commander-
in-Chief, Exzellenz v. Scheer. And it was with the greatest
joy and enthusiasm that I received his permission.

A small, old torpedo-boat, used as a despatch-vessel between
Wilhelmshaven and Heligoland, brought me to the German
North Sea island. There, in the U-Boat harbour, lay the old
Sophie, which was used as living quarters by the U-Boat
officers. I was already expected, given a most friendly welcome
on board the still smart-looking old vessel, and shown to a
very bright and roomy cabin.

U-Boats of various types and sizes lay against the piers—

some of them ready for sea, others just returned from a successful voyage. A few grey torpedo-boats, too, were sojourning as
guests in that U-Boat realm. Their characteristics were not
dissimilar, and men were frequently transferred from and to
them.

In the large and airy ward-room of the *Sophie* the commanders and officers, modest men with much war experience,
used to meet together. When, with the shining eyes of
youthful enthusiasm, they exchanged their experiences in
their own simple words or sat smoking and absorbed in stale
illustrated papers at the long mess-table, it was hard to believe
that this cabin housed the harsh reality of the mighty struggle.
How much of the best of Germany's loyal, gay, confident
youth had foregathered here ! How many had left that
peaceful-looking harbour with their comrades and their
trusty boats, and sailed away westwards and northwards—
never to return !

The numbers and the types of the vessels changed, and new
crews were constantly arriving ; but the confident spirit, the
iron sense of duty that knew no rest, remained unchanged.
Here were no pirates nor Huns, whose sole emotions were
brutality or joy in murder. They were defending our just
cause and our beleaguered land, fighting for their hard-pressed
comrades on shore. Like sharp, cleaving knives these small
grey boats persistently cut through the enemy's stronghold in
just and justified retaliation. What the enemy did, it must
also be our right to do.

How calm and peaceful looked the North Sea round the
island ! The great guns in the casemates had never fired a
shot in anger. But Heligoland, now evacuated by the population, and inhabited only by the Navy, was fully equipped as
an advanced post in the war-area.

But why stay here and merely watch the U-Boats come in
and depart ? My observation and admiration of all these
mine-layers and U-Cruisers in this placid harbour was not
enough to give me a clear picture of their activities. I must go

out with them and share the experience. My thoughts and
desires dwelt more and more on such a possibility. " Come
with us, then," said a young Lieutenant of a mine-layer U-Boat
under orders for the east coast of England. " We are going
quite close to land : you could see a great deal." But the
Commander of that boat had no room for a visitor. Or were
there other reasons ? Others advised me not to go. " What
do you think you will see or paint ? Once you are started you

There lay a large boat of the Fifty class just back from a long voyage.

will be under water all the time and see nothing." It might
be so. I could not answer this question myself. But my own
ignorance of the reality could not satisfy me. All I could do
was to wait until a favourable opportunity offered.

One hot day in early summer a large submarine of the
Fifty class, just returned from a long voyage, lay beside the
U-Boat pier. The huge conning-tower—not unlike a Roman
war-chariot—and the gun, were covered with red and orange
rust ; the sunburnt crew were full of their recent homecoming,
and in all the glow of youth and health. I sat down to paint
the graceful vessel, and I soon had a number of spectators in

black, brown, salt-stained, oil-gleaming leather jackets. The Commander came across the gangway on to the quay, walked up to me and cheerily introduced himself. He smilingly asked me about my work, and wondered if painters, too, got their hands dirty. Indeed, there was no doubt about that.

"Then I daresay you can make good use of a piece of real French soap that we have brought back with us."

The U-Boat's eye.

I thanked him and took the precious gift.

"And I expect you get hungry, too?"

That was not exactly true; however, I gladly accepted the apple preserve and a tin of American corned beef that he offered me. Both had come from a steamer he had sunk. Although our rations on the *Sophie* were ample and excellent, such things meant a change that was unknown at that time. Moreover, his kindly spirit made me feel warmly grateful.

The boat went out for the trial dive. I went on board its escort so as to be able to observe the individual phases of that manœuvre from close at hand across the water. In a few seconds the low-lying hull, the gun, and at last the conning-tower, had disappeared in a bright eddy of foam; then the topmost section of the glass-eyed periscope cut through the greenish-blue water in front of a narrow strip of foam. One ceased to be aware that somewhere near-by beneath the water, a long, slender vessel, with crew, engines and torpedoes, was carrying out a test attack. Suddenly the quickly lengthening track of a torpedo sped directly towards us. It would have been a certain hit. The smoking eel finally came to rest some distance out to sea and waited, swaying peacefully on the waves, for the escort-boat to pick it up. Then the tall periscope, the dripping conning-tower, the gun, and finally the whole vessel, emerged with magical unexpectedness above the surface. Commander and officers came out on the conning-tower and waved across to us. The Commander semaphored a kindly invitation to me to dine with him that night in the club on the upper island with his comrades and officers.

Wonderful, indeed, is the atmosphere of the clear blue moonlit night on the terrace of the club, with its far-flung view across the glittering, sleeping sea. Over a good glass of wine I asked the genial Commander whether he would not sometime take me for one of his long trips on his U-Boat. Without much hesitation he discussed the pros and cons of the matter with his three officers, sent a wireless message to the Admiral in command of the U-Boat service at Wilhelmshaven, got the consent of his Navigating Officer and Warrant Officers as regards accommodation, and informed me next morning that there was no further obstacle to my accompanying him, on my own responsibility, if I still felt so disposed. Thus, sooner than I expected, I had the long-desired opportunity of a voyage on a U-Boat. I quickly sent to say that I would come, got the necessary U-Boat outfit, and was soon ready with my modest baggage.

A few weeks before, unlimited U-Boat warfare had been declared, and the voyage promised to be interesting. After dispelling a few doubts (and a violent attack of cold feet), I went on board, stowed my belongings in my bunk above the Navigating Officer, inspected my utterly unfamiliar surroundings, and waited for the next event.

With its new light-grey coat of paint glistening in the sun, the boat lay alongside the pier, ready to put out to sea. The

Commander briefly explained to the crew, before they went below, the object and destination of the voyage. They were to lay a course north of the Shetlands to the entrance of the North Channel and the Irish Sea, and there carry on operations off the north-west coast of Ireland ; thence cruise about the western entrance to the English Channel and the south coast of Ireland, where determined counter-measures on the part of the enemy were to be expected. The gangway was pulled on shore, the ropes cast off ; brief words of command rang out from the conning-tower, from which a flag was fluttering. The boat quivered as the engines began to revolve. Shouts of good-bye, waving of caps, silent farewells. Amid cries of " Good-luck ! " the vessel glided slowly towards the harbour mouth, and out between the two lofty moles, on which a few comrades stood and waved good-bye once more, into the green, gently heaving North Sea.

The boats headed north, past the Hog-Steen-Tonne, so well known to all who sailed on U-Boats. The red-rock island gradually vanished into the distance. A new world seemed to have arisen before my eyes. It was refreshing and pleasant on deck and in the conning-tower, in the light sea-breeze of this glorious clear sunny weather. The almost level dark wooden deck, nearly 50 metres long, provided ample opportunity for movement, though on the smaller mine-laying submarines there was little possibility of stretching one's legs. After a great deal of stumbling about and clinging to the rails one soon became accustomed to the various square holes in the deck that catch one's boot-heels, and to various other pitfalls ; indeed, one quickly finds one's sea legs on a U-Boat. There is time and to spare to contemplate at leisure the details of the 10·5 centimetre gun that stands in front of the fore-hatchway, the tall conning-tower welded with myriad rivets, and all the other equipment of a U-Boat. The ubiquitous and plentiful oil and grease make little impression on the admirable leather overalls worn by U-Boat crews. Only linen, hands, drawing-paper, and suchlike more genteel objects

The red-rock island gradually vanished beneath the horizon.

soon lose their original purity. One smokes quantities of cigars and cigarettes and talks to the genial members of the crew about their earlier experiences.

A German fishing-steamer came into sight and hove-to at once : U-Boat and steamer were soon lying side by side. The steamer Captain, an old friend of our Commander, passed several baskets of freshly caught fish over on to our boat ; indeed, his generosity seemed endless. The deck looked like a fish market. Above and around screamed and hovered countless seagulls in expectation of a copious feast. The men were soon busy over the fish ; the best ones were sorted out, washed, cut into pieces, and handed down in buckets through the fore-hatch into the tiny U-Boat kitchen. We offered our warmest thanks to our kindly friends, and after much waving of caps the two vessels parted. Whole flocks of sea-gulls swept the sea clean behind us from the remains of the fish that we had thrown overboard. Above our heads circled two escorting aeroplanes. Their presence had a very com-forting effect, for, in spite of the reassuringly peaceful fish transactions, dangers threatened us on every side. Enemy submarines might even here be on the watch. But on our boat, too, up on the conning-tower, several pairs of sharp-sighted falcon's eyes were always keeping watch for suspicious streaks of foam, periscopes, and similar unwelcome signs of attention on the part of the enemy. In front of us steamed two patrol-boats fitted with mine-sweeping apparatus, formerly steam-trawlers, and guided us through the mine-strewn zones of the German Gulf. When we had turned our course to starboard, and passed the long gleaming dunes of Sylt, the North Frisian island that rises still and dreamlike on the far horizon from its grey-blue background, the two fishing-boats turned back and their place was taken by two torpedo-boats. The aeroplanes, too, were later on relieved by two seaplanes, until further north, on the edge of the German sea-zone, signals and flares indicated the departure of our brave guides and companions. With a message of " Good-luck ! " torpedo-boats and seaplanes turned back in the light of the evening sun. We are left to ourselves. In the distant haze, beyond our wake, the torpedo-boats disappear, and the 'planes quickly vanished from our sight in the direction of List, on the island of Sylt. The engines are at full speed. Sharp and noiseless our bow ploughs the heaving sea. Northward speeds our ship ; she has seen much service, having made her

There were always several pairs of sharp-sighted falcon-eyes keeping watch from the conning-tower.

way across the Atlantic to Newport and back after a stormy voyage of many weeks, and through the blockade-line from the Shetlands to Norway.

After an excellent supper on the fresh fish given us by our fisherman friends, we were glad to clamber up the conning-tower to enjoy the northern evening air and a cigar. The sun had already set behind England ; grey and violet hues and the silvery gleam of water replaced the shining glow of sunset. But it remained light for some time. We passed in silence, and at some distance, two solitary German patrol-boats, far out on the high sea and, like us, dependent on themselves—a hard and heroic service. Several German deep-sea fishing-boats glided phantomlike past us in the twilight. They do not seem to realise the risks of the naval war. What do they care for the enemy, or for mines? So long as there are fish in the North Sea they will catch them. Without that spirit there would be no ships and no trade.

For days we did not see a ship. Only driftwood, baulks and planks, intended originally for the construction of enemy trenches, and now, in contradiction of the proverb, that water is not planked over, swinging on the North Sea tides; perches for contemplative seagulls. From time to time a bale of cork, a small piece of wreckage thickly encrusted with mussels, came into view; and occasionally a rust-covered mine adrift from its moorings. For the rest, nothing was visible but indifferent sea-birds, and the almighty majestic sea, careless of the disputes of insignificant men whose ships it tolerates upon its waters. Communications by sea were cut. Was it the blockade or the German U-Boats? The latter, more probably. Onward to the north, to the broad ocean where the great transport-ships in huge convoys carry munitions, war-material, and troops for the destruction of our land and people. Here is no hunting-ground for us in this silent North Sea, the zone of the great war-vessels.

The rhythmical beat of the motors hammered on without a pause. Some of the crew who were off duty lingered on deck to enjoy the strong sea air and to smoke. Yes, if there were nothing to smoke, the voyage would have been wearisome indeed. All were silent, deep in their own thoughts. Our wake disappeared in zig-zag lines into the twilight behind us. From time to time the officer on the watch would shout orders for a change of course through the open hatchway to the helmsmen in the conning-tower. On each side of our bows the clear blue-green sea surged past us in white racing eddies.

The sea grew rougher, waves began to break over the deck, and swept foaming across the oil-glistening iron-black curved and barrel-like outer tanks. From bow to stern, over the two masts fixed to either side of the conning-tower parapet, run two stout steel hawsers which serve as protection against nets and as antennæ for short-distance wireless, when circumstances do not allow of the erection of the tall wireless mast affixed to the diving-tank outside. The flag has long since been taken in, and every object that might cause inconvenience when moving under water has been removed. Several periscopes, heavily cased in grease, respond to the lightest touch, for at any moment an alarm may force us to dive. I had had my first experience of this on the first day of my first U-Boat voyage, at the trial dive, which was not merely to prove the boat's diving capabilities, but also served as a pleasant occasion for the award of the extra allowances to the crew that are given for every dive.

" Diving stations ! " The order suddenly rang out from the conning-tower. In an instant the deck was empty. Everyone jumped, climbed, or swung himself on to the conning-tower ; and thence down the open hatchway. The tall periscope is soon in its place. Quickly down the smooth iron greasy ladder ; and don't let the great seaman's boots above you crash on to your fingers ! And mind your head and your bones in this iron tube, plastered with iron plates, levers, screws, and wheels, and now crammed with scrambling men. In less time than it takes to describe, everyone from on deck has dashed to his appointed place, inside the conning-tower, in the control-room, or in one of the other compartments of the vessel. Last of all the Commander climbs into the conning-tower and the heavy hatch is fastened above his head. The oil-engines are switched off and the electric motors started. Just as the Commander stands at the periscope in the conning-tower, the eye of the U-Boat, so in the control-room, the brain of the vessel, the Chief Engineer stands at the centre periscope. One's tense expectation of a unique experience, and all the impressions of one's first dive in a U-Boat, are mastered by the amazing consciousness that here one is, in a huge heavy ship, shut up in it unescapably with a number of other men, sitting on a comfortable leather sofa in the little ward-room, or in the control-room, watching the sailors at the horizontal rudders and the depth-gauge, in a brightly-lit dry compartment with pounding engines and a row of eel-smooth torpedoes, moving under the surface of the sea.

I can clearly discern the bow gun hovering in the magical green light.

The alarm bell rings shrilly through the vessel after the report from the conning-tower : "Conning-tower hatch closed." The levers spin round : with a hiss and a roar the sea pours into the diving-tanks ; it seems as though one ought to feel the weight of this invading water. Gently the floor sinks and the boat tips forward. The movement is quite gradual, barely perceptible. In the dim glow of the electric light, a mystic modulation of various shades of grey, stands a figure, enclosed in a narrow iron space surrounded by all manner of levers and wheels, on a sort of pedestal, connected with the periscope, that can be raised and lowered like a lift—the Commander at the periscope, which is now fully raised ; and in front of him the helmsman at the wheel. With the Commander's permission I open the heavy iron safety-cover of one of the small side windows and press my face inquisitively against the thick glass. There in the light of day, as though in another world, I see the foaming masses of water crashing over our bows. The gun disappears in surging eddies. The waves rise and race towards us, break angrily against the conning-tower and sweep past my window. Then a confusion of bright foam and clear water, inaudible, fantastic, outside the glass : light grey, dark grey, the deep water grows ever darker and more calm. I can clearly discern the bow gun hovering in the magical green light. The sunshine pierces the clear water and glitters on the polished steel. A solemn stillness reigns. The adjustment of the periscope and the movement of the submarine steering-gear are the only sounds in the vessel that are audible in the conning-tower. The Commander uses both hands to swing the greased and glittering periscope, now dripping with water. In his eye, the only eye in the vessel that is still in communication with the upper world, is the bright and shining reflection of the light of day. I swing back the iron cover to my window, leave the narrow tower and climb down to the control-room, where an officer stands in charge of the horizontal rudder.

When the order " Surface stations ! " is given, the Chief Engineer superintends the blowing out of the diving-tanks by means of compressed air. This manœuvre involves an infernal din of hissing, roaring water. The boat lifts. From time to time the Engineer gives me a glimpse through the central periscope, and I see the bow and the gun rising through the surface slime. The whole deck is at last clear. A slight shock in my ears ; the conning-tower hatch is open again and the fresh sea-air streams into the boat. The movement of the water becomes again perceptible, the stillness of our progress through the depths has vanished. The sea rustles past the hull. The oil-engines begin to hum once more. Thus our first dive came to an end.

On the conning-tower everything was dripping with sea-water. Fragments of jelly-fish and strips of golden yellow sea-weed were hanging from the steel hawsers. Behind the conning-tower casing the look-out men, enveloped in yellow and black oilskins, stood like statues, immovable. The long, keen sight of these experienced seamen is almost beyond belief. Much depends on their alertness, and any weariness, careless-ness or mistake might be fatal. The safety of the boat and the crew is in their charge. It is only their iron calm and experi-ence that prevents them constantly seeing ghosts of periscope tracks in the little bright dancing eddies, or behind the sweeping lines of foam. And seagulls, too, balanced on the moving water, are very apt to lend themselves to such deceptions. The look-out men can recognise with the naked eye the smoke of a completely invisible steamer by the merest suspicion of a shadow on the horizon as quickly as they can spy the needle-like line of a mast in the far distance. Before I could detect the smoke or the masthead with a pair of strong binoculars, the alarm was given.

It was cold up on the conning-tower with the look-out men. The boat was speeding towards its hunting-grounds. We had still a long way to go before we reached the Atlantic to the west of the British Isles. Below, in the small but cosy ward-room, with its homelike wooden panelling, in such refreshing contrast to the iron world about us, the officers ate their excel-lent and varied meals prepared in the electric kitchen. We were very comfortable on the soft black leather sofas, which, when hung at night with dark green curtains to help to keep out light and movement, served the officers as beds. In this excellent abode we soon got used, as our voyage progressed, to the most gracefully acrobatic methods of consuming our food and drink : here we sat and passed from hand to hand some ancient novel, or an illustrated paper so old that it had lost all verisimilitude ; and we found it easy to transport ourselves in spirit out of that iron vessel, the war, and the sticky sea-water, to peaceful shores and homely familiar towns and cities. The small library in the Commander's room, the accumulation of many kindly gifts, was assiduously used. Immediately adjoining the ward-room, and communicating with it by a door that was always left open when we were proceeding under water, was the smaller living-room and bedroom of the Commander. He ate, as is the custom on all warships, alone. A small writing-table, covered with photographs and all sorts of maps and sailing directions, served also as a dining-table. I was, incidentally, allowed to use this as a work-room. Between the Commander's cabin and the control-room there is a small wireless cabinet, equipped with all its mysterious apparatus. Near-by is one of those strong rounded bulkhead doors, armoured and covered with levers, leading through a tubular passage to the somewhat less cramped control-room ; but before passing through it one should bend down and be careful to remember that iron is always harder than one's head. A similar alley-way joins the control-room to the oil-motor room behind it. When the intruder opens the great riveted armoured door into this complicated domain of marvellous technology he is assailed by a deafening din from the precious Diesel engines. The noise of the pounding machinery is so terrific that only shouts have any chance of reaching the engineers, wedged among their levers, wheels, and a hundred technical devices which a layman cannot understand. It is a little hell of rattling, whirring tumult. Every screw is watched, and not the slightest irregularity in the rhythm of the engines can escape those experts whose ears are attuned to noise. Everything is dripping with thick grease. In this place no cold air can penetrate. In the next compartment, which is the home of the heavy electric motors that drive the boat when it is under water, in contrast to the domain of the oil-engines, there reigns an almost solemn stillness, as also in the other compartments, except for the now somewhat hoarse but treasured gramophone rasping out ditties of home, or the sound of the compressed air whistling into the diving-tanks when the boat rises to the surface. A smooth greasy iron ladder, about $2\frac{1}{2}$ metres long, leads from the electric engine-room through a hatch, just large enough for one man, on to the after-deck, to the daylight and the fresh sea-air.

Right astern, and also forward in the fo'castle, lie the torpedoes, the gleaming, red-tipped, death-dealing, precious " eels," the dreaded weapons of the U-Boats. They are all still aboard, waiting for freedom and their prey. They cramp the quarters of the cheerful leather-clad ratings, who crouch in their bunks and hammocks above, below, and beside the firmly packed carcases of the torpedoes. In this continual half darkness details are difficult to distinguish. Here is true comradeship,

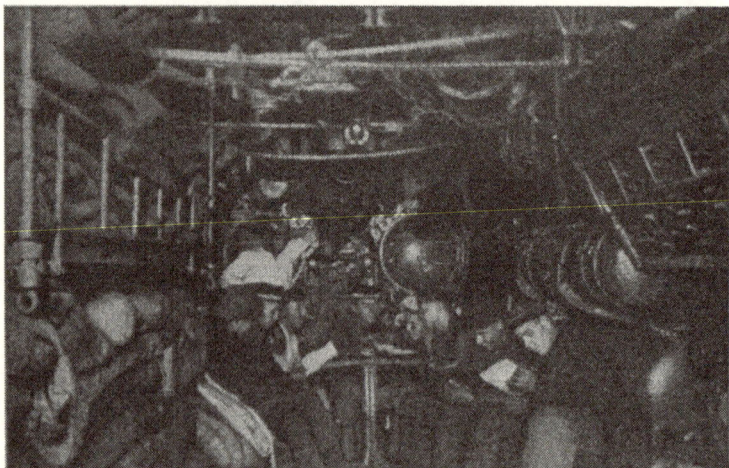

A U-Boat forecastle ; home of true comradeship.

tempered by an iron regard for duty. These men never utter a murmur, or a word of complaint at their hardships ; indeed, they have no time for that. At their post of peril on the ocean, with death continually lying in wait, they think of nothing but the service of the Fatherland, like true German seamen and soldiers. The U-Boat crews are loyal to each other, to their boats and their officers, until the end. Borne up by such a spirit and guided in this sense, the crews of the German fighting U-Boats lived and worked, feared and therefore hated by the enemy.

I carefully push aside my green curtain and assure myself by a glance over the edge of my bunk, so near to the curved steel roof, whether the Navigating Officer below me, one of the most important persons on the boat, is still asleep. This officer's repose is sacred. However, this morning he is sitting on his bed, in his leather clothes, with his legs in his sea-boots, eating his breakfast ; I can get a bird's-eye view into his smoking coffee-can, and breathe the pleasant odour of that meal. Then, with an agility to which I am now accustomed, I swing myself on to the floor. There are only sea-boots to put on, for the rest of one's clothing is worn, day and night, during a voyage that may last weeks. Thus, one's toilet is extremely simple, if not particularly thorough. Indeed, washing and shaving are seldom practised of a morning. It becomes easy to study the luxuriance or otherwise of our respective hair and beards. Probably the real pirates of old days looked much as we do ; but the inner kernel behind this rough exterior does not justify any further comparison with that dreaded rabble of the seas. Water and soap are very precious on board a U-Boat. Morning cocoa and bread and marmalade taste delicious under such conditions.

The alarm bell shatters the morning repose, and brings with it the order : " Diving stations ! " The ship is suddenly full of hurrying men. The look-out men come crashing down from the conning-tower and report an English destroyer to port, whose masts, high bridge, and several funnels were already visible. When so much of one of those nimble sea-hounds can be seen above the dip of the horizon, it is high time to dive. She is bearing down on us with the speed of wind. But either this, our first, enemy did not detect us, or she lost the track of us when we dived. We were soon on the surface again. Nothing could be seen of our lively morning visitor. During the next few hours we kept an even closer watch on the horizon, which was successively obscured with haze, or veiled by a succession of squalls. Very soon after, a second suspicious vessel approached us from the port quarter and then quickly

c

vanished. These northern waters seemed to be growing gradually more animated, and we could already feel the presence of the enemy. However, we were not alone in the fight. Our wireless operator reported to the Commander, who was on the look-out in the conning-tower, the receipt of a wireless message from a German U-Boat between the Orkneys and the Shetlands, with the gratifying news that she had sunk 40,000 tons.

. . . firing with one eye at the periscope.

Such successes were by no means rare since the beginning of the U-Boat war.

An enthusiastic reception with special festivities awaited the successful crew of every boat which could report more than 30,000 tons sunk. But what it meant to reach such figures, what terrific hardships, nervous energy, endurance, calculation and foresight were needed, and in the face of how many insistent perils such results were achieved, those not initiated cannot imagine when they read the bare report : " So many thousand tons sunk in spite of powerful resistance by the enemy."

I had opportunity enough to convince myself during this long U-Boat voyage how incredibly difficult it was, after calculations and manœuvres that might last hours, to carry out a successful attack and get in a position to fire a torpedo at a ship protected by fast, well-handled, heavily armed escorts.

And even at that point came the art of accurately firing the costly instrument after only a second's aim, with one eye, through a periscope constantly dipping up and down with the movement of the water and thus cutting off the field of vision. If the periscope, that was used so cautiously and rarely appeared above the surface, or its inevitable trail of foam, or the course of the moving torpedo, were discovered too soon by the enemy, the chance of success was gone. The enemy, too, was very experienced in the arts of defence, in attack, in deceptive manœuvres, and in steering zig-zag courses that were very hard to calculate. On all the enemy's surface vessels there were many practised eyes on the look-out for U-Boats ; they were set upon our destruction, and there were tempting honours and rewards for every success. What with their U-Boat chasers, destroyers, aeroplanes, nets, depth-charges, U-Boat traps of all kinds, U-Boats, and many other devices, they pressed us very hard. There were mishaps on both sides that for many meant the end.

I inquired of the Navigating Officer on the conning-tower what our position was, and learned that we were roughly in the latitude of the southernmost point of the Shetland Isles. We had to set a widely encircling course to the north round these islands so as to reach the Atlantic and, ultimately, our more southerly scene of operations. We had still a considerable voyage before us. A shorter route would be between the Orkneys and the Shetlands, past Fair Island ; but for various reasons it was not chosen on this occasion.

In spite of the summer season, in the cool wind that blew across this wide expanse of sea we felt nothing of that heat that we had found so exhausting in Heligoland harbour. With dry decks the slender vessel rose and fell on the long rollers. The steel-blue sea seemed to be heaving deep breaths. The Atlantic began to make itself felt. The great, powerful and majestic movement of that ocean replaced the lighter and more agitated currents of the enclosed North Sea. The blockade line was behind us. Where, indeed, was that blockade? The single destroyer? That, surely, was not much. A vast feeling of relief came over us all. Suddenly in the far distance a U-Boat came into sight. How small the grey object looked in that expanse of ocean ! In response to our wireless signals and flares, she reported herself as U 58. Our own people once more. So the German U-Boats ruled the seas ! In a short time the two very similar looking vessels stopped at a certain distance from each other. Both crews swarmed up on

Friends again !

to the conning-towers, all eager to witness this happy meeting. Besides, all sailors are rather inquisitive. The Commanders communicated without difficulty by means of the so-called " whispering bag " : they exchanged some important information, and the two boats then separated with much waving of caps and shouts of " Good luck ! " In a few minutes our friends had vanished once again as though the whole incident had been a dream.

A rising wind made the sea rougher. Waves began to break across the deck. The weather became cloudy and visibility was very limited. We reached the northernmost point of the Shet-

The Commanders megaphoned to each other.

lands, and therewith the Scotland–Norway convoy-route.
Now we might expect to see steamers, sailing-ships, and vessels
of all kinds. In the ward-room that day there was a small
glass of brandy and a cigar for every man in celebration of the
fact that we had reached the northernmost point of our trip.
The conning-tower soon looked like a pleasant open-air club
as the smoke of those excellent cigars rose upon the air. Late
in the evening we talked to U 54, which came pretty close to
us, on her way home from the Bay of Biscay after sinking
19,000 tons. Hereabouts, in fact, there were more U-Boats
than enemy ships. When the watch was relieved, the setting
sun conjured up the most magnificent colour effects on the
clouds and the heaving sea. The fiery ball of the midnight
sun hung, as it were, against a bright red wall. Dark violet
tufts of cloud, rimmed with gold, drifted across the red blinding
disc. It seemed hardly to approach the horizon, and when an
hour had passed, it was almost at the same level. Just as I
was carrying below a sketch of this marvellous spectacle that
I had made under some difficulties on the conning-tower, the
sun at last sank below the waters. But the rosy glow remained
on the horizon all night, and another day soon dawned.

On the starboard side, a few yards off the diving-tank, a
large black three-cornered fin, belonging to an apparently
sleeping shark, emerged from the sea. The noise of our propellers as we passed did not seem to disturb the monstrous
creature. In that transparent water we could clearly discern
the vast size of the sea-pirate. I saw many other such three-
cornered fins, on more than one occasion, alone or in company
with others. Another age-long war beneath the surface of
the sea.

In grey weather, among the high Atlantic rollers, with a
following wind, we pursued our course southwards. We had
passed the northernmost point of Great Britain. Heavy
breakers swept over the plunging boat. Enveloped in thick
oilskins, with sou'westers pulled down over their heads, and
wearing their heavy sea-boots, the look-out men were at their

posts on the pitching conning-tower. The gigantic greenish-blue waves towered mountainously behind us. Like a glacier, they heaved forward under the foaming broken water of our wake, raced along the lower deck, and surged with an ominous roar in heavy translucent masses against our point of vantage. It was not yet rough enough to crouch under the conning-

Enveloped in stout oilskins, the look-out men were at their posts on the pitching conning-tower.

tower casing, or to make it necessary to lash the look-outs to their places. The vessel rode swiftly through the mountainous seas. The level monotonous line of the horizon disappeared ; the high tossing waves cut off our field of vision. The periscope was raised above the conning-tower like a glittering mast, so as to enable the Commander to see as far as possible. Several enemy fishing-boats were labouring through the heavy seas, which made it impossible to fire at them. This time these poor hens escaped their fate. When an especially heavy breaker hit the side of the boat there was a crash of glass or mess-traps in the fo'castle or the ward-room. Some agility and caution were needed not to be flung heavily against the iron walls of the boat as one made one's way about. However, as soon as the warmth of the Gulf Stream made itself felt, although the weather did not improve, it was pleasanter to stand in the somewhat confined space of the conning-tower in the fresh sea-air than to remain below.

Our eyes and ears and leather kit were coated with white salt ; and my black leather coat gradually assumed a lighter hue, to my own and the Commander's satisfaction, since, upon the sight of an enemy smoke-cloud, I, as a dark speck upon the conning-tower, had perilously increased the boat's visibility. I could now without objection crouch behind the casing and watch manœuvres. In fine weather the usual wear was a grey sweater that had once been white. Time and circumstances themselves suggested the colour-protection mimicry both for boat and crew.

Enemy smoke-clouds now began to be more frequently sighted. Two patrol-boats were also recognised. They all vanished without a trace.

A new day of bright, refreshing sunshine broke over the green waters, and the sea grew calmer. Shortly after breakfast, about nine o'clock, several smoke-clouds appeared to starboard. At first, only two masts of a steamer were visible, continually shifting as a result of the vessel's zig-zag course. Half an hour later the larger of the three vessels was clearly recognised through the periscope as a merchantman, accompanied by two patrols, steaming at top speed on a zig-zag course and under cover of thick smoke-clouds, through the blockade zone to its port of destination. The Commander decided to follow her. The conning-tower then became crowded. On a large sheet of paper, with the help of two T-squares, a pair of compasses and a pencil, the Navigating Officer traced the enemy's observed course, which the Commander then checked on his bearings apparatus. Every movement of the vessel was watched through strong binoculars.

After some time and calculation the Navigating Officer was at last able to estimate the steamer's direction and speed. It was now our task to get ahead of the enemy vessel as fast as possible, or, in other words, to cut her off, and ourselves to remain unobserved. Fortunately a black cloud of smoke is always visible at a greater distance than the relatively inconspicuous conning-tower of a grey U-Boat. At last everything was ready for the attack. At this point, another U-Boat, to which we had sent a call, appeared upon the scene. After a mutual understanding as to the possibility of a combined action, both boats dived to attack the now fast approaching enemy.

Checking the enemy's course.

Then began the nerve-racking hours of under-water navigation. The Commander kept unceasing watch on his victim through his skilfully handled periscope ; the oily water, that trickles in through the crevices round the periscope, dripped down over his cap and face. The reflection of the daylight shone brightly in his keen blue eyes.

Below was the silence of the grave ; only the sound of the horizontal rudders broke the uneasy stillness. Every man was

at his post, waiting for any orders that might come. I was
sitting in the Commander's room at his writing-table and
listening through the speaking-tube to the reports from the
conning-tower : " Now she's turned again," or " One of the
patrols is coming straight at us," or " The steamer's got a
gun on deck." No one moved. The bulkhead doors and the
heavy iron hatches were closed. The gun crew waited in the
ward-room, and discussed the position as the moments passed.
The most important question was the supposed size and
tonnage of the steamer that was approaching our torpedo-
tube. Then once more we heard the sound of the periscope
chain as it shifted up and down. We seemed to have been
waiting an eternity : we stare into vacancy and wait. Everything depends on the Commander's judgment and ability.
Would the enemy sight our periscope ? Would the patrol-
boat manage to head us off just before we fired ? However,
after manœuvres that lasted several hours, on this occasion
some mishap defeated us and made any further attempt hopeless. The steamer had somehow become aware of our presence
and turned away at the last moment ; but the U-Boat that we
had met had then fired at her. We stayed for some considerable time at a depth of 20 metres with our periscope lowered.
When we rose, our conning-tower had hardly appeared above
the surface when the patrol-boats and their charge, now far off
but still visible, opened rapid fire on us, but without success.
While we could see the jerking flashes of several guns to one
side of us, a new cloud of smoke appeared ahead. This time
it was a large tank-steamer. " Diving-stations ! " Once
more we plunged into the shelter of the blue-green depths.

An attack offered no prospect of success, so that after an
hour we came up to the daylight once more. A destroyer
which appeared on the scene later did not observe us. As a
result of these failures we were all in rather low spirits, but hope
of better luck soon restored us to our usual good-humour.
Now began a conflict with the natural forces of the sea. U 53
fought her way bravely through the raging waves ; for two

days and nights she pitched and rolled in the tumult of the waters. More than once the vessel seemed to be plunging into an abyss ; then followed a crash and a quiver of the whole hull, when a watery mass stormed down upon the boat and flung her plunging bow upwards once again. All night long without ceasing, the furious waves could be heard smashing on to the decks and racing off the outer tanks. One had to wedge one's arms and legs most uncomfortably against the iron walls and partitions so as not to be flung out of one's bunk. Washing and eating were indeed a test of skill. In this fury of the elements we had nothing to fear from the enemy ; he had enough to do to look after himself in such weather. But even this turmoil had an end, and the sea grew calm under a clear blue sky. Soon a cloud of smoke appeared—a large English auxiliary cruiser painted grey, with high deck-structures. She had sighted us and bore down in our direction. Suddenly she turned and opened fire with several guns. We hurriedly dived, and at 30 metres were safe from her shells. We had found our way into a much-frequented and patrolled area. Time after time smoke-clouds came into view. In the far distance appeared a U-Boat that did not answer any of our signals ; she was English, and quickly disappeared. Strange that the enemy should sail the sea in U-Boats that he so detests when they are German.

In the ward-room one of the officers was shuffling a pack of cards to predict the outcome of our next attack. Sailors are always superstitious. Besides, this sort of prophecy is not always wrong. We are now outside the entrance of the North Channel to the Irish Sea, a highway of the great Transatlantic steamers. An alarm soon followed, and we dived ahead of a gigantic creature, guarded by two destroyers, coming in from the Atlantic. Their speed was far too great to give us any possibility of manœuvring into a position for attack. And regretfully we watched the 24,000-ton Cunarder make her escape. It would have been a good catch.

Shortly after, U 61 came alongside us, on her return home.

The two long slender boats rode softly on the heaving rollers.
A magnificent and heartening picture. We are, indeed, the
masters of the sea.   U-Boat after U-Boat, far out at sea, in
enemy waters, close to the coasts of our adversary, like a girdle
round our enemies, in defiance of them and their unscrupulous
blockade that was to cut off our subsistence.

Fine, calm weather, after heavy storms and much under-

U 61 came alongside.

water navigation, once more gave the crew a welcome chance
to stretch their legs on a dry, warm deck. Some sat with
their legs in the warm water as it streamed past, enjoying a
refreshing foot-bath. Others engaged in physical exercises or
in the crude if jolly sport of " ham-slapping." I decidedly
preferred my *rôle* of passive spectator or artist to this somewhat
exacting amusement. A large school of porpoises leaped in
elegant curves round our bows and stern : great fat fellows
with black gleaming bodies and white bellies. Then a
frightened flock of little bright-coloured puffins fluttered

awkwardly over the waves. The denizens of the high seas are very various and attractive.

In such peaceful observation war and destruction are almost forgotten until the merciless alarm-bell put an abrupt end to Nature study, and recalled us to the deadly seriousness of U-Boat activity in the blockade zone. The closing hatchway shut the lovely sunshine out of the iron chambers. We lay at periscope-depth awaiting a steamer that was approaching on a rapid zig-zag course. The torpedoes were ready in the outer tubes. Then the Englishman suddenly altered course and bore down straight upon our periscope, which he had meanwhile detected. He was trying to surprise and ram us. Only about 50 metres separated his sharp and menacing bows from our periscope. Calm and resolute, our Commander grasped the danger, which in a few nerve-racking seconds he averted by diving hastily to a considerable depth. The thudding of the steamer's propellers was clearly audible above us. There followed a deafening explosion, and a crashing blow that made the whole boat quiver. The glass of the depth-gauge was smashed. The lights went out. The emergency lighting was soon turned on, and in unshaken calm and discipline measures were at once taken to deal with the damage. The horizontal rudder

Fine, calm weather gave us a chance to stretch our legs on the dry, warm deck.

mechanism was out of action and seemed to be jammed. The boat was moving at a considerable depth. A second and third less powerful explosions followed quickly. Depth charges ! All of them above the boat. Thank heaven, none of them had hit us. The horizontal rudder apparatus was soon put in order and all was well. The oil-tanks were undamaged, and thus all trace of us was lost to our cunning adversary. Many a U-Boat and many a Commander, however successful and daring, might well have found a tragic end in such a situation. The conning-tower hatch was open once again. With joyful grateful hearts, with radiant happy eyes, each and all of us, now that the danger was past, saluted the glorious sun as though it had been a fresh gift of God. We had come very near to death, but—we were still alive.

Forward ! By the evening there were again several smoke-clouds on the horizon. After an hour and a quarter's cautiously calculated manœuvres, the order rang out : " Diving stations ! " We were not to enjoy the daylight for long. After two further hours of anxious movement under water we were ready for an attack upon a large steamer, escorted by a small black armoured patrol-boat. The nervous tension had reached its limit when at last the longed-for order came down the speaking-tube and brought us deliverance. " Let her go ! " Our first shot with a torpedo. The deadly missile left its tube with a jerk and sped through the water. All eyes were glued on the slowly moving second-hand of the clock, intent and anxious.. Fifteen . . . twenty . . . five and twenty seconds had passed. Now ! . . . A dull far-off crash shook the boat. A hit ! If one could only see or know something of the tragedy that was being played out on the water in those moments. They are, perhaps, the last seconds of life for many human beings. The Commander hurriedly sent for me to his peri-scope in the conning-tower. No sooner had the unsuspect-ing escort passed us, than the torpedo tore its way through the iron walls of the great steamer's stern. In my brief glimpse at the bright reflection in the lens I saw the vessel already sinking,

The bow pointing to the sky.

the bow pointing to the sky, a red hull, thick white steam bursting from the funnel, a few crowded lifeboats, the helpless escort standing by, waves glittering in the bright sunshine, an English White Ensign. Then I had to make room for the Commander. Scarcely had I got down to the ward-room again than I heard : " She's sunk." The periscope was lowered, and we proceeded under water for a long time so as to keep out of the way of the destroyer which the sinking vessel and her escort had summoned by wireless. Lloyd's Register was now consulted as to the probable size and name of the steamer we had just sunk.

It was not until about midnight that we came up again. Through driving clouds the moon casts her cold silver radiance on the phosphorescent sea, which has grown rougher in the interval. The water pours across the deck in myriad flashing green and blue pearls of light, and behind us the greenish-white silver band of our wake shines like a gleaming pathway. Great glittering masses of iridescence surge up to the surface of the waters. The look-out men stand motionless on the conning-tower, like dark shadows. Their faces, wet with sea-water, shine eerily in the bright green reflections on the sea.

The boat was slowly making her way towards the place where the steamer was sunk the day before. In the grey light of morning we could see far off on the tossing waves an apparently endless deposit of oil on which were floating hundreds of variously coloured barrels, pieces of wreckage, balks of timber, and other *débris* of a holed and shattered steamer now lying 4,000 metres beneath the surface of the sea. This expanse of oil, glittering with all manner of colours, lay like a great shroud over this ocean grave. In oilskins and sea-boots, with hatchets and axes, the crew were on deck and searching among the floating casks and timbers for any object that might give any indication of the name of the torpedoed ship. An oar was sighted and quickly fished out of the water ; then a red lifebelt. The latter was inscribed in white lettering with the

. . . an apparently endless deposit of oil on which were floating hundreds of variously coloured barrels, pieces of wreckage . . . .

steamer's name and port of origin. It is entered in Lloyd's Register as 10,402 tons, from Liverpool. What was the cargo ? What was in all those casks ? After much labour a few were dragged on to the deck. Thick brown oil trickled from the blue barrels : the red ones were packed with completely solidified whitish-yellow stearine. Hundreds of such barrels of both kinds were floating singly or in masses on the oily waters. Many were broken open or smashed. Glorious oil and fat ! The rough sea prevented us from salving any part of this precious cargo. The oil would, of course, have been most useful for our motors. The contents of a single barrel of stearine was broken up with hatchets and taken below ; then we left this strangely fascinating place of ruin, and the oil-smoothed heaving waters, the scene of a tragedy of the war.

Soon we were alone once more on the clear blue sea, that still flashed with greenish iridescence. Higher and higher towered the long rollers and raced down upon us as we thrust on our way. Salt foam swept once more over the conning-tower and the gun, and whipped against the thin oilskins of the look-out men. It was refreshing to stand there on the little iron fortress in the middle of the raging ocean, in the driving rain and biting spray. We thus reached our intended station near what had been reported to be a much-frequented enemy trade-route. However, for two whole days neither masthead nor smoke-cloud broke the line of the horizon. It was, of course, to be expected that our presence and our destructive activities had been reported by wireless in all directions of the compass. The only vessel we saw was a far-off English U-Boat chaser dashing through the sea. These extremely fast vessels, armed with guns and torpedoes, constructed specially to deal with German U-Boats, were, from their great speed and their consequently unexpected appearance, very dangerous adversaries. Then, by way of a change, we sighted two English vessels simultaneously, both steaming very vigorously, one towards England and the other out to sea. We attacked the outward-bound vessel with our gun. She put on full steam ahead, while she tried to shake us off by rapid fire from her stern gun ; but it was badly handled and her shots fell short. Unfortunately, her far greater speed prevented us keeping in touch with her.

A very different spectacle met our eyes on the following day when a black tank-steamer hove into view ahead. Quite slowly, with very little smoke, and no attempt at a zig-zag course, the ungainly oil-ship lurched on her way. She seemed unarmed, for the closest inspection did not discover any signs of a gun. Was she really so completely defenceless against U-Boat perils in the blockade zone, as to steam through it with almost suspicious innocence at the very point at which a large steamer had been sunk only a few days before ? The torpedo hissed out of the tube. Straight as a taut cable sped its greenish-white wake towards the centre of the steamer. Now ! . . . Twenty . . . twenty-five . . . thirty . . . thirty-five seconds, and still no explosion. It must have hit ! But the steamer was still calmly afloat. It was now clear that this was no harmless tank-steamer, but a U-Boat decoy, fitted with a deceptively deep draught and possibly ballasted with cork. The Commander did not take his eye off the suspicious vessel for a second. Suddenly she stopped, blew off some white steam, and expeditiously lowered her lifeboats, which had been swung out before the attack, fully manned into the water. She had observed our well-aimed and well-intentioned torpedo, which had unfortunately missed and gone under her keel. Orders soon came down the speaking-tube to rise to the surface and man the gun.

The conning-tower hatch was opened. The greasy iron ladder quivered and clattered under the hasty tread of several pairs of sea-boots clambering upwards. Men with unshaven stubbly beards, sou'westers tied to their heads, yellow oilskins, and set faces with their usual confident expression, shouldered their way past the Commander's little platform up to the light and the gun. In a few minutes our first shell was screaming its way across to the apparently abandoned tank-steamer. A tall grey-green pillar of water shot upwards quite near her bows. The two lifeboats still kept the same distance from their ship, which seemed not yet to have been entirely abandoned. Admirable innocence !

Our Commander drew a little nearer to the enemy, so that better aim could be taken as the sea was rather rough. Suddenly the harmless steamer turned and got under way again, moving at right angles to us. At the same moment the mask fell. The decoy opened a well-prepared broadside from quick-firing guns. Nearer and nearer came the shots. Shells whistled over our heads and splashed into the water. If only our tanks were not hit ! With iron calm our gun-crew bore their part in this artillery duel. In the meantime the lifeboats, containing the supers in this unwelcome surprise performance, had rowed round to the lee of their ship and were being taken on board again. The actual gunners, revealed at last and firing savagely, had, in malicious expectation of the success of the trap, been lying on their bellies beside the hidden guns. Under continual fire from the pursuing decoy we managed to draw out of the enemy's range. Urgent S.O.S. calls soon brought two English destroyers to the spot, which forced us to dive and made it impossible for us to defeat our adversary ; but we subsequently learned that on another occasion she joined others like her at the bottom of the sea.

A school of porpoises, disturbed by the unfamiliar splashes of the falling shells, or, by way of celebrating the strange performances, indulged in the drollest acrobatics between the two ships while the fight was proceeding. One of the grandest, as well as the most inexorable and terrible, qualities of the sea is its indifference to the incidents of human conflict. It admits of no recognisable or enduring scars of a battle, and the changing yet eternal face of the ocean reveals nothing of the fates of men and of their ships that for so many thousand years have vanished in those impenetrable depths.

We were still enjoying the cheerful and invigorating sunshine in spite of our late mishap, when another destroyer

With iron calm the gun's crew bore their part in the artillery duel.

forced us to dive hastily. One after another we scrambled below ; the heavy conning-tower hatchway fell with a dull crash over the last head. A few seconds later, as I glanced through the periscope in the control-station, I could see nothing but blue-green water, from time to time a bubble dancing upwards, strips of seaweed, quivering fragments of jelly-fish hanging from the steel hawsers, or the water streaming

Artillery duel broken off by a crash dive.

in silver threads over the conning-tower casing or against the stout periscopes. We lived in two separate worlds—in the one, bathed in the purest sunlight and the clear air of the vast limitless ocean ; in the other, enclosed by glittering fathomless blue-green waters in a cramped locked iron cabin on a diving-boat.

The reddish-gold rays of the setting sun lit up the gleaming boat as it rose out of the foam with its blue-grey conning-tower flecked with orange-red patches of rust. The crew were soon crowding on to the streaming decks to stretch their legs a little, but a curt wave of the arm from the Commander, in his black oilskins at the periscope above, soon drove them below again. Another destroyer. These are the pests that compel us to travel under water. This was her third appearance that night. A very persistent creature. However, we kept below for some time and she lost track of us.

After many hours under water we were glad of the morning sunshine and a rest on deck. Suddenly another destroyer came dashing up. These fellows seem determined on thoroughly testing the diving capacity of our U-Boat. This time, however, it was an American. Our Commander recognised her unmistakably through the periscope by her construction and her flag, and observed with a laugh : " One of my friends from the Nantucket Lightship " ; in the days of American neutrality their searchlights had been useful to him when he was sinking a few steamers off the North American coast.

To-day their attitude was notably different. With a whirr of bells, their pounding propellers dashed over our hull ; then through the steel walls we heard the dull explosions of a whole series of depth charges. No damage done. The enemy pursued us until darkness began to fall. The fact that he was able to follow our course made us wonder whether one of our oil-tanks had not sprung a leak. He was, of course, well aware that we must inevitably come up when our batteries ran out.

The cautiously raised periscope revealed the American's masts and smoke as so far distant that it was thought we might venture to the surface under cover of the falling darkness. An unbroken dark wall of mist and rain only too easily conceals our watchful foe, to whom our silhouette against the background of a brighter evening sky must be clearly recognisable as that of a U-Boat. But our look-out men's practised eyes can pierce the shadows lying on the sea. During this critical night we prayed for the moonlight to preserve us against surprise. At last the clouds began to roll back and the bright disc appeared. But what a singular change ! It was dark orange in colour, dull and lifeless, completely obscured by the shadow of the earth ; we were witnessing, in fact, a total eclipse of the moon, a phenomenon of which we had heard, but had never before seen, and, unfortunately, it was taking place just at a time when we were waiting for bright moonlight. Had the moon conspired against us ? or was she, in the spirit of true neutrality, helping us by declining to provide our enemies with any searchlight service ? The latter was the most probable, for, though we did not relax our vigilance for an instant, we were able to watch all the phases of the eclipse undisturbed. The ancient patroness of seamen thought, no doubt, to preserve us from pursuit by veiling her face. Then, when the shadow of the earth had passed from her silvery countenance, with kindly anxiety and perhaps a touch of malice, she slipped behind some gathering grey-black clouds from which burst hissing squalls that covered our vessel in impenetrable pitchy darkness. The middle watch between twelve and four received orders to keep a specially sharp look-out. Their eyes and senses had to be kept clear and calm so that they might see any phantoms in surrounding blackness. Only the dawn brought us relief and certainty that there was no enemy near by.

We set our course north-west against heavy seas and rough weather. Storm-lashed foam-flecked waves dashed against our bows. The whirling spray swept like eddying dust over the tumult of waters. Defying the wind and rain, flocks of pitiful-looking little puffins, with their white-striped heads and reddish-yellow beaks, wheeled and fluttered round us, fleeing before the grey iron ship, on which they had noticed some human beings very strangely disguised. The terrified little creatures were on some mysterious journey as they soared over the blue-green crystalline edges of the waves and the snow-white scattering breakers. Vast dazzling foam-fields broke on the toppling billows and swept in smooth strips or in myriad white flashes into the green hollows. Our thrusting bows shimmered like emerald in the clear Atlantic water. When one has learnt to look out for the more powerful waves that dash against the conning-tower and cover one with spray, it is simple to crouch under the casing, draw one's head in like a tortoise, and let them burst and pass. Everywhere is clattering steel and streaming water. Carefully guarded in the hollow of one's wet hand is the glowing stump of a sputtering cigar. Perhaps all this is the sign of Neptune's favour. Drawing in such circumstances became a form of sport—the gift of snatching at a dry interval which may not last a second. One's left hand clutches a dirty oil-stained sketching block, while one's right, not much cleaner than the left, in the intervals of wiping off the sticky salt spray, tries to make a few notes and sketches on the precious paper. Work of this kind is truly art. Any paper that will endure such treatment, and any sketching-block that does not dissolve in its first sea-bath and is not ripped in pieces by the tearing wind, is indeed commendable. My materials stood the test. Every sketch, every note, everything in fact that one brings home after such weather, are gracious gifts of the elements. When all is said, constant observation and study are the only means of describing events and experiences later on with any semblance of truth. No artist can ever succeed in capturing, with the dead paints on his palette, that marvellous play of colour, the light-effects on surging towering waves, the deep transparencies of the sea, or the shifting dazzling contrasts of light and shade—revels of reflected sunlight. We can do but little. In the face of such majesty of Nature and the splendour of such movement we are almost helpless. Only recollection, the sense of great experience, and the training of the eye and mind, can help an artist in his portrayals and interpretations.

We gradually arrived off the northern corner of Ireland in the neighbourhood of Lough Swilly, a fjord-like inlet running deep into the land. Beyond, in the hazy distance, the mountains of the Emerald Isle rose some 2,000 feet above the sea. Against this lovely background moved a fully-rigged ship

A sailing-ship held up off Lough Swilly.

under sail. Our first sailing-ship ! Allowing for the possibility that this might be a U-Boat trap, the Commander opened fire at a distance of 4,000 yards. Breakers were dashing over the entire fore part of our vessel, much embarrassing the gunners, who were lashed with ropes and belts to the gun and often up to their hips in surging water.

After the first few shots the crew of the sailing-ship took to the boats, and one of them laboriously made its way alongside the U-Boat. Several men, wearing the most diverse garments and unseamanlike headgear, clung to the benches of their boat as it danced on the waves like a nut-shell, casting timorous and questioning looks at the German blockade-runner, and especially at the gun trained on their ship, which was now hove-to and which they still appeared to think might be spared. They answered in English the Commander's question regarding the origin, cargo, and crew of the ship, which was sailing under neutral colours. It was Norwegian, on its way in ballast from Dublin to America with a crew of twenty-four men. A

The end.

gesture from the Commander conveyed to them that they were dismissed and had better join their comrades in the second boat, which was now some distance off, and make for the coast of Ireland off which we were lying.

One shell after another tore great holes in the Norwegian's hull below the water-line. At every hit the whole rigging quivered, and great clouds of dust and powder floated up through the sails and spars high above the masts. A quarter of an hour later the proud sailing-ship, now full of water, began to move, turned uncertainly, and once more ran before the wind. Her stern was now noticeably down in the water. Her sails flapped : still struggling against her end, she turned once more, and, swaying several times to port and starboard, quivered and sank by the stern, almost majestically, with all sails set. A light green eddy, strewn with barrels and woodwork, marked her place of disappearance, from which a few minutes later loose timbers shot up out of the water. Nothing was now between us and the view of a long chain of mountains, though again an approaching destroyer prevented any more prolonged enjoyment of the lovely coast-landscape. Through the periscope which the Commander allowed me to use for a while, I could clearly distinguish the entrance to Lough Swilly between Dunaff Head and Fanad Head opposite the lighthouse ; the shapes of Raghtin More and Slieve Snaght were clearly visible, and, in the bright sunshine, the rich green meadows dotted with a few houses near the shore. A turn of the periscope revealed more mountains. Behind us, to the west, lay Tory Island. A few steamers and smaller vessels could be seen making their way along close in shore. For six long hours we lay under water, steadily patrolling between Fanad Head, Horn Head, Tory Island, and Bloody Foreland ; we learned later on in Heligoland that a few days before a German mine-laying submarine had deposited its entire cargo in these waters, in which, all unsuspecting, but thanks to our good luck, we had manœuvred without damage. It would have been a bitter end to be sent to the bottom by German mines.

A little pale as the result of our long sojourn under water, we came up to the refreshing warm sea-air. Sharks, seagulls and all manner of sea-birds enlivened air and water during our further journey through the entrance to the North Channel towards the southernmost of the romantically isolated Hebrides islands off the west of Scotland ; and the solitary St. Kilda group in the Atlantic was expected to come into view that day. Outside the North Channel several other under-water attacks similar to those already described, were carried out, some with good, and other with less satisfactory results. I, of course, saw little of what took place. All the torpedoes had been fired except one, and the tonnage figure of the sinkings did not yet satisfy the Commander. For this reason he was not yet disposed to sail for home. After all, we had an excellent gun, and might well expect to make good use of it some time. Such was the tenor of our conversation at luncheon that day when the look-out men reported that the high rocky outline of St. Kilda was coming into view on the horizon.

I was soon in the conning-tower. I had long wanted to see St. Kilda and had been anxious to make some studies there before the war ; well, I was now able to do so under strictly limited conditions. So I stationed myself with sketch-book and pencil as comfortably as I could against the rivet-studded steel casing of the conning-tower, to make some notes of what I saw. Nearer and nearer came the rocky home of the myriads of birds, large and small, that sail over the deep-blue waters. The individual groups of islands began to be distinguishable. Gradually, to a height of several hundred metres, the rugged reddish-grey cliffs, worn by the great Atlantic breakers, rose up perpendicular from the sea. On the precipitous slopes are grassy meadows on which are pastured a race of hardy sheep whose excellent wool has long been world-famed. A few smaller rocks stand up like towers out of the breakers in grotesque and jagged isolation. The graceful outline of the main island, St. Kilda, is now visible. Beyond it, a lofty cone of granite, like the dome of a cathedral, crowns the whole magnificent panorama ; it belongs to the island of Sevenish. Further on is the third group, Soay. It must be inhabited by myriads of large seagulls and other birds, for little else is visible but a scurry of white wings. A scene of wild and splendid natural beauty. These granite islands lie in the middle of the ocean many miles away from the mainland.

Communications with the nearest islands, the Hebrides, are bad and not always feasible. When the furious storms of

. . . the graceful outline of the St. Kilda group.

winter roar across the Atlantic, life must be full of hardship and privation. The largest of the islands, St. Kilda, after which the whole group is named, possesses a small harbour and a few small stone hut-like dwellings that house the population of some seventy unfortunate souls. The islands of Soay and Sevenish are the domains of birds. The conspicuous white lime-like deposit on the rocky pinnacle is guano that has been untouched for many thousand years. Bird-catching in the almost inaccessible rocks, and the weaving of the much-prized brown and white wool on the primitive spinning-wheels, are the chief pursuits of the inhabitants besides sailing and fishing. Many whalers call in at the small harbour on their way to the far north ; indeed, in these very waters we saw the unmistakable blowings of these great sea-mammals. And eternally, in leaping foaming breakers against those stubborn granite walls, beats the besieging sea.

But . . . we are not here for the study of natural phenomena or the enjoyment of the landscape. Ahead of us, to starboard, a white sailing-ship was trying to out-distance our pursuit. With full speed ahead we managed to overhaul her ; and a few shells induced the fugitive, a fine-looking ship under a neutral flag, to heave to. This time, too, the crew hurriedly took to the lifeboat and made for St. Kilda under sail. Suddenly there appeared round one of the rocky headlands two thick clouds of smoke, and, shortly after, the shapes of two armed patrol-vessels, which must have been stationed at St. Kilda, and which the sound of our firing had just reminded of the object of their hitherto aimless existence. We could already see the distant flashes of small guns. However, it was now essential to sink the sailing-ship quickly before any of their shells should damage our tanks. A direct hit had already set the vessel on fire amidships, and from it came bursts of reddish flame and thick clouds of brown and sulphur-yellow smoke. The sea poured in through the side of the ship in such volume that, at a distance of about 50 yards, the magnificent creature sank with all sails set in a very few minutes. Only the imperious necessity of sinking every ship within the blockade zone could master the grief natural to every true seaman at the sight

A direct hit set the sailing-ship's saloon on fire.

of the destruction of so splendid a vessel. But, in this matter, beauty and poetry were as nothing against our duty to the

Fatherland. If we were to starve like rats in a trap, then surely it was our sacred right to cut off the enemy's supplies as well. Moreover, the declaration of the blockade zone was no mere menacing phrase, but an evident reality of which it might be truly said : He who enters into danger shall perish therein.

The helm was put over hard a-port. Without alteration of course we soon outdistanced our labouring pursuers, who were still energetically but vainly bombarding us, and as we rounded the romantic island group the noisy little creatures disappeared from view. For a long while we watched the sunlit St. Kilda rocks shining across the waters under the clear northern evening sky, flecked with pink clouds ; and later the desolate Flannan islands appeared in a reddish glow to port. A notable day, rich in material for an artist, was drawing to a close. Northwards again !

A new day revealed to us, far off on the horizon, and partly obscured by heavy clouds, the jagged dark outline of the distant Danish Faroe Islands. The long low rollers reflected the strange clear light of the turquoise-blue transparent northern sky, severed from the sea by a hard straight horizon-line. Against a distance that seemed almost infinite, eight smoke-clouds stood out, well defined and within range ; they belonged to a little steamer flotilla steaming northward. Our trusty Diesel engines drove the boat swiftly onwards, and our bow ploughed the greenish-blue water into almost palpable walls on each side. The heavy fishing-vessels could not escape, in spite of all their efforts to reach the protecting waters of the Danish island-group. Rightly realising the hopelessness of the race, they tried to shake off the pursuer by an ingenious device. They divided into two sections, steaming in a line, an armed guardship bringing up the rear of each ; in this way our boat, as it plunged forward in pursuit, was brought under concentrated fire, which, however, fell short. Our gun, set at a high elevation, fired alternating shells and shrapnel at both vessels, which were clearly recognisable by their white funnels and the English ensign as armed trawlers. The others sought safety in flight. Bursts of yellow and black smoke showed that our fire was proving effective ; but the patrols fought obstinately and bravely. We drew nearer. The enemy shells splashed into the water only a few yards from our bows, and began to scream over our crowded conning-tower. I smoked a cigar and sketched. The patrols then drew together and began a well-directed rapid fire. Shortly after, a burst of black smoke rose high over one of the steamers whom we had christened the "Admiral." A series of hits followed in quick succession. She now tried to escape under the sulphur-yellow clouds of her smoke-bombs, but her wild zig-zag steering brought her outside the veil of smoke as it moved obliquely across the water, and with every turn she offered an excellent target of which we took full advantage. They had soon had enough. Steam was pouring from their funnels. They stopped, and hurriedly manned and dropped their lifeboats. On approaching these shabby-looking black vessels where they lay pitching on the rollers, we saw the guns with their armoured shields hanging over the port bulwarks, completely wrecked by direct hits. Hanging by ropes over one of the guns was a boat-shaped object painted black which had served as a range-finder. So these oily fishing-tubs had been ready, when opportunity offered, to assume the part of U-Boat decoys ; and on that day their destiny was sealed. The shells tore their way through the thin iron hulls with dull booming crashes. The "Admiral" sank bow foremost in the usual way ; her consort vanished silently by the stern. The pressure of air and water flung a little black cloud of soot from the funnels of both, the so-called " black soul," the final farewell of a steamer on its way to the bottom of the sea.

. The other six trawlers, which were still in flight, were soon overtaken and stopped. Six more lifeboats left the abandoned ships that lay scattered about us, none of which was equipped with wireless. We could proceed to sink them without fear of disturbance. Two of them were destroyed by gun-fire and the four others by high explosive cartridges. Our "prize crew" in the small dinghy, the only small boat we had, were fully occupied with collecting various items of cargo that seemed likely to be useful to us, and with fixing the explosives. Six times the same performance was repeated ; between the time the explosive was placed in position and the sinking of the ship, I made, as we passed, sketches of six dirty-looking steamers, each of them with a high bridge close to the funnel, two short masts, and their ports of origin and rather pompous names painted in white upon their hulls.

We were alone on the broad sea, except for six small black points away to the north rowing to the isles of refuge. A strange and unforgettable scene was taking place on the fore-deck. The crew in their leather kit, and among them the officers keeping strict order : on the deck a medley of boxes and chests of cocoa, coffee and expensive tea, sacks of wonderful American meal, fresh butter and globes of margarine, cordage, unused nets, oilskins, rubber boots that did not fit the crew, fine white English bread, English marmalade, ham and bully-beef, bacon and beans, two bars of good soap, tobacco and various oddments. All these things, which were now completely strange to us, we had removed from a few paltry enemy fishing-boats, while in Germany the women and children were starving and dying of inanition, or supporting life on vile, injurious, almost uneatable food-substitutes. The poor in Germany thought of old days as they sat over their watery turnips ; while in the cabins of these trawlers, which we happened to have sunk just at dinner time, were plates piled with, what seemed to us, lavish helpings of good fresh roast meat and potatoes, such as we only saw in dreams. No one was allowed to touch these appetising meals for fear of poison. The stores, which would be useful to us and much appreciated at home, were stowed away below. Then, setting a wide course round the Shetland Islands, we began our homeward journey to the North Sea.

There was a strange light in the evening sky. The sun had long since set, but the whole circle of the horizon was glowing with a fairy-like red splendour—a natural phenomenon that we could not explain. Our contemplation was cut short by a seal's desperate fight for life that was taking place near by. Again and again the poor creature leaped right out of the water to escape its pursuer, a clearly discernible large shark. It was soon over : the greedy monster grasped its wretched victim between its sharp teeth and disappeared.

We were now leaving the blue depths of the Atlantic, and the shorter waves and greener water betrayed the neighbourhood of the North Sea. Once more we had to pass the English line of blockade, but once more we did not see it : only one large steamer painted with red and white stripes, and clearly marked with the sign of safe conduct. We stopped her ; there could be no exception for neutrals, even, as in this case, for a Swedish boat. The handsomely painted badge of neutrality, so often abused by the enemy, had for a long while been no guarantee for a ship's good faith and peaceful intent. The seas were full of U-Boat decoys cunningly tricked out in various disguises. From the signal-mast over our conning-tower fluttered the international flag signal : "Bring your papers on board"; and the gun was manned and cleared for action.

The other vessel must have seen the signal, but she showed no signs of paying the slightest attention to the orders of a U-Boat. Did she take us for an English submarine ? A shell plunged into the sea near her bows and flung up a tall pillar of water—an argument that appeals to the thickest-headed seaman. An answering signal appeared on the steamer. Good ; but she did not diminish her speed, nor did her captain appear to be taking any steps to lower a boat. A second shell splashed into the water in front of her. Another signal went up : "Can't recognise your flag ; give us a wireless call or come nearer." A third shell was the reply to this impudence. Finally she stopped and sent a boat. We drew off a little to give them the pleasure of some more rowing exercise. The boat, with the steamer's first officer, slowly came alongside. He

The boat, with the steamer's first officer, came slowly alongside.

was at first very reluctant to come aboard, but at length he obeyed the Commander's instructions, and, with a great black portfolio under his arm, clambered up to the conning-tower, where the Commander and the Navigating Officer were waiting for him. He shook hands heartily when it was at last clear to him that we were Germans ; and he answered our questions in excellent German. His ship was on her way from America and had been detained six months in Falmouth, and was now upon her return journey to Gothenburg, in Sweden. When it was pointed out to him that they were in the blockade zone and exposed to the risk of being at any moment sunk without warning, he relapsed into speechless astonishment. His eyes lit up with gratitude when the Commander, with an urgent warning to get out of the blockade zone as soon as possible, told him that his ship could proceed. He assured us that, whether we liked to believe him or not, they had not seen a single English war-vessel during their entire voyage. He got into his boat again with every appearance of satisfaction and waved us a cheerful good-bye. He no doubt informed his passengers of the chivalrous behaviour of the U-Boat Commander and his crew, for they all cheered and waved to us as we passed the steamer. It is to be hoped that she got safely home.

Our course was south-west in the direction of the island of Utsire, on the Norwegian coast. The tall long-distance wireless masts which had been rusting peacefully on the diving-tanks were now erected, and soon provided us with important news from home and from enemy countries. We were very glad to be in contact with the world again.

Next day the lofty snow-covered Norwegian mountains and fjords, glowing in the delicious morning sunshine, came into view. Within the three-mile limit, beyond the risk of U-Boats, several sailing-boats and steamers were moving along the coast ; and, through our glasses, the clean painted houses, the white windows, gleaming roads, wireless masts, and ships lying in the harbours, were clearly to be seen. Under a distant cloud

of mist lay Stavanger. All who were off duty went up on deck
and watched the passing panorama. For a whole day we sailed
along an ever-changing mountain landscape until, towards
evening, it dipped into a broad coastal plain. Then we
reached the Skagerrak, a name that holds so many proud
and gloomy memories. Here, twelve months before, the two
mightiest fleets on earth fought the greatest sea-battle in history.
Here, friend and foe had lost many glorious lives and splendid
ships. But this vast battlefield will never betray the secrets
of that great day, no crosses or flowers mark the last resting-
places of many heroes who lie in their riddled and shattered
steel coffins under the keels of the countless ships, full of joyous
laughing passengers, that shall pass above their heads in years
to come. And, just as those heroes lie upon the sea-floor in
the Skagerrak, many thousands more lie in their sunken
vessels scattered round the coasts of Europe. In appeasement
and protection the eternal sea spreads its waves over all those
brave sailors.

A rough sea and a stormy night accompanied us through
these heroic waters. Were they the spirits of our sleeping
comrades that greeted us in the salt spray and howling gusts
of wind ? The boat was swung sharply round, as the breakers
dashed over us once more. We had been notified that the
great U-Boat and mine area began at the Danish coast, which
we were following at the three-mile limit. We were ordered
to put on our swimming-jackets. The Captain humorously
commended the excellent Danish cooking and the good clean
hotels in case I had to swim ashore that night. The closed
bulkheads made the ship feel like a gigantic mousetrap.
During the early hours of the night I listened for any suspicious
sound outside the hull. One waited—though one did not
hope—for the ominous iron grating sound of a mine. In point
of fact, it would then have been far too late for any lengthy
reflections on how to escape from so unpleasant a proximity.
However, a sound sleep was the best way to get rid of such
futile speculations. Next morning, with the deep and joyous

consciousness of being still alive, we hailed the daylight, the German North Sea, two German torpedo-boats, and German airmen.

Our comrades came to meet us, just as they had escorted us on our way. Morning coffee and a good cigar tasted delicious. Everyone was busy cleaning himself up—washing, shaving, and hair brushing—for we did not want to enter Heligoland harbour looking like pirates. A wonderful peaceful summer day greeted our glad clean faces, radiant at the thought of home. The Commander of a torpedo-boat fitted with mine-sweeping apparatus that came to bring us in, flung us a hawser, on the end of which was a watertight tin box attached to a red lifebelt, containing fresh tomatoes for the ward-room and a bundle of rather stale newspapers. However, it was hardly to be expected that torpedo-boats on such remote service, that often lasted for days on end, should be able to produce the latest journals. Besides, what did we want with newspapers? Signs were quite enough to answer our mutual questions and to exchange the latest news of war and home. A few German patrol-boats and an outgoing U-Boat hailed us. The green North Sea stretched away in front of us as smooth as a mirror. Seagulls from our own land circled above us and followed our wake. To port we could see once more the long shining dunes of the North Frisian islands. At last the shout: "Heligoland in sight ahead!"

The torpedo-boats that have escorted us into safety now turned back, after being heartily thanked by our Commander. Nearer and nearer came the familiar red rocks, and about midday the harbour gave us joyous welcome. A large number of U-Boats great and small were gathered there, the old *Sophie* signalled a welcome, and officers and men on the U-Boat quays waved greetings to their comrades on their safe return after a four weeks' voyage.

For me, as a painter, the voyage had been rich in experience and instruction, and now it was over. I would not have missed a day or an hour of that voyage in the company of my U-Boat

At last the shout : " Heligoland in sight ahead ! "

CLAUS BERGEN

comrades, whether in the cramped compartments of the boat, or with the look-out men in the conning-tower, in blazing sunshine and on a mirror-smooth sea, or in the wild surges of the storm-lashed Atlantic. Once again I thank my companions of all ranks, and especially our incomparable Commander, that I was privileged to see the reality of the U-Boat warfare that we carried on so chivalrously.

When I felt the soil of Heligoland beneath my feet once

Conning tower of U 53.

more, I had first of all to answer the question that had been asked me before I sailed, " Did you see anything ? " A fragment of the struggle, on the sea and under it, had come to life before my eyes, and I had seen so much and collected so many impressions that my pen, like my brush and pencil, can never set them down.

The comradeship of the U-Boat men and the picture of the magnificent U-Boat 53 are memories that will never fade out of my mind.

2

MY FIRST U-BOAT VOYAGE (SEPTEMBER, 1914)

By

Engine-room Artificer Karl Wiedemann

IMMEDIATELY after war broke out, England's policy of blockade by sea made it manifest that her aim was the economic strangulation and starvation of Germany. Swift counter-measures were essential if Germany were not to lose the war almost before it had begun. The Naval Authorities recognised in the U-Boat an effective instrument against the hunger-blockade established by England. It is true that there were not, as yet, enough U-Boats ; and the Naval Authorities devoted their utmost efforts to remedying this shortage.

At the beginning of September, 1914, the first volunteers for U-Boat service were taken from the Torpedo Division of the Fleet. Together with a number of my comrades, whose only thought was to get at the enemy as soon as possible, I reported at once ; and I passed the Medical Examination.

" Fit for Service ! " I shouted, and already saw myself out on the high seas in pursuit of English steamers and sailing-ships. But that was a little premature ; and I had to resign myself to stay at home for a while and learn my work. It was a severe trial of patience.

Two days later, I and my comrades who had also been passed as fit for service were transferred to the ship where the prospective U-Boat crews were quartered ; and we were set to work on the boats lying in dock. Dock labourers ! It was rather a disappointment to me. While the skilled workmen hammered, nailed, riveted and filed, we had to undertake the odd jobs.

I boarded my first U-Boat—the U 19—with true sea-manly pride and self-satisfaction. But when I saw the boat's mechanism I began to feel rather less confidence in my abilities, and I envied the regular members of the crew. However, my enthusiasm for U-Boats restored my courage and strength : I was eager to serve my Fatherland in any way I could upon such a ship. And the succeeding days proved that I was quite equal to my duties.

U 19 was ready to put to sea. I had taken part in all the tests that are carried out a few days before a long voyage to ensure that the boat neither lists nor leaks. At the prospect of my first submarine voyage I felt a glow of eager joy.

The U 19 was to start on the following day. My delight was beyond expression. Suddenly, however, we were dismissed from the boat, and in a state of utter dejection I led the working-party back to our old quarters.

The second disappointment !

Darkness fell : supper was over ; we all sat and stared moodily into vacancy, unable to shake off our depression. In the late evening the Warrant Officer in charge of our quarters came into our room—probably, I thought, to take a final look round. " What does he want with me ? " thought I, when he suddenly stopped in front of me, told me to pack my kit, and report at once on the U 19. Hurrah ! Radiant with delight, and envied by all my comrades, I took my departure.

Next morning we put out to sea. The Chief Engineer was very kind and gave me an instruction-book on U-Boat manage-ment, which I read and studied in all my free time. My new comrades were fine upstanding fellows, seamen of long experi-ence, some of them silent and sparing of speech, others talkative and noisy, but every one of them proud of his seamanship and muscle.

The first watch, that passed without noteworthy incident, was over.

After supper we were allowed, in turns, to go out on to the upper deck and smoke a cigarette. When I went up, the

Commander, Captain-Lieutenant Kolbe, told me to paint out the large white figures on the side of the hull, so that the enemy might not discover the boat's number. The work was quickly done, and I was soon back in my bunk reading my instruction-book. One of the crew urged me to come on deck with him again, but I would not ; he amused himself with some indifferent occupation, which did not last long, for he was soon snoring heartily. A sudden crash soon awakened him from his wholesome slumbers.

What was it ? The boat was listing to starboard : the alarm-bell rang persistently and the Commander ordered us to diving-stations. We had not yet reached our various apparatus, when a second frightful crash threw us off our balance. Every object that was not secured to its place was flung in confusion on to the floor. Guns were thundering near by and the glare of a searchlight flashed through the conning-tower.

" Stand by ! Lifebelts and swimming-jackets : every man on deck," the Commander rapped out in a calm, determined tone.

My position was not at all agreeable, for as an extra member of the crew I had neither swimming-jacket nor lifebelt ; there was nothing for it but to stay below and wait for the end. I went along to the control-room and found my friend the Engineer : there at least I was not to be alone, while the rest of the crew hurried up on deck. Suddenly the order rang out : " Both engines full speed ahead : get ready to dive." The crew stumbled down the conning-tower again, we did a crash dive, and were soon—it seemed to me like a dream—lying on the sea-bottom.

Then the crew began to exchange experiences of what they had heard and seen. An English torpedo-boat destroyer, invisible in the darkness, had struck us heavily on the port side. Hence the first crash. When the destroyer was right on to us, both Commanders had given the order " Hard over," and the two hulls crashed together. Hence the second shock.

Calm was soon re-established. The Chief Engineer shouted to me to join him in the control-room, and asked me what I had thought at the time. " That's the end of that," was my reply. He laughed and gave me a bottle of schnapps.

When we came up to the surface in the early hours of the morning and the danger was past, we were able to ascertain the damage to our vessel. The port torpedo-tube and the head of the torpedo were completely cut through, the anchor-housing smashed, and the cable torn off. We had to abandon our programme of a long voyage and turn back home.

When the boat lay in dock at Wilhelmshaven, it was found that there was a good deal more damage of varying importance. It was especially difficult to extract the two broken parts of the torpedo-head from the tube.

I, however, was delighted to have been on my first U-Boat voyage and to have come through it without mishap.

3

CHRISTMAS AND NEW YEAR, 1914–1915, ON U 24

By

Engine-Room Artificer Nikolaus Jaud

U 24 was lying in harbour at Wilhelmshaven, and it did not seem likely that she would put to sea that day. A dozen or so dock-hands were working on board with compressed-air hammers mending a leaky petrol-tank. The interior of the boat looked like an old iron shop—hammers, files, drills, and machine parts all lying about in inextricable confusion.

The stokers gradually reduced the engine-room to order : I pushed the last matey through the central hatchway, and we were our own masters at last.

The engines had to be tested before we left harbour. The two oil-engines were turned on by an electric switch. When the pressure of the oil and of the water in the radiators were found to be in order, the ignition was tested. The cylinders started with a roar, driving the motor like a dynamo. The din in the engine-room was terrific ; it drowned any attempt at speech, and communication was only possible by signs.

The running of the engines was carefully noted : the ear grows quickly accustomed to the Diesel rhythm, and, in spite of the noise, the slightest irregularity can be detected. When the cylinders had been tested the engines were switched off. The test was over.

" Clear for action ! " We all hurry to our stations.

The engine telegraph rings, and the vessel moves slowly from the quayside. We were soon through the lock gates and slipping along the Jade to the North Sea. Both oil-engines needed the greatest care : first one, then the other, cylinder would misfire. However, it could not be helped—they had to serve.

The north-west wind grew stronger : we were in for a storm. Every object was secured to its place, and every aperture, including the conning-tower hatch, was closed. The last patrol-

The sea soon became unpleasantly rough, and the boat laboured against the heavy waves.

boats disappeared, and we were without outside help, utterly dependent on our own resources. The sea soon became unpleasantly rough, and the boat laboured against the heavy waves.

My friend Romulus relieved me, and I told him to keep an eye on the port engine oil-pump, which had fallen out of action shortly before. A wave of his hand signified that he had understood me, and I was able to lie down in my bunk. Karl Wegner sat down on the edge of it and told me various news.

He didn't appear to be tired, and it was only my entirely selfish advice that he, too, had better get a little rest that broke off the conversation. I tried to sleep, but it was not so easy. Outside, the night bellowed and raged : the boat rolled unpleasantly, and the crashing of the waves beneath me made my bunk wretchedly uncomfortable. I wedged my knees against the side and the small of my back against the edge of it so as to lie a little at ease.

A sharp order shook me out of sleep. I rushed into the engine-room to my diving-station. My chief duties were to attend to the main bilge-pump, the regulating-tanks, and the speaking-tubes in the fore and aft compartments. Orders were already coming through the speaking-tubes ; the signal lamps were turned on ; the regulating-tanks were flooded and the automatic ventilator in the conning-tower opened. The Chief Engineer stood with both elbows on the gyro-compass and directed the diving manœuvres. The boat plunged downwards. Forty-five seconds after the first order the boat was at periscope-depth—11 metres. From the conning-tower came the order, " Dive at full speed." The regulating-tanks were flooded with half a ton of water, and we were soon 25 metres beneath the surface. An enemy vessel had sighted us and compelled us to dive. The Commander gave his instructions in the engine-room for the passage under water, and those not on a watch were able to lie down again.

Next morning the weather was better ; the air was clear, and there was less wind. Nothing could be observed through the periscope, so we came to the surface. The entire day passed without any noteworthy incident. As night came on we sank to the bottom again. The next day was Christmas Eve and we wanted to be undisturbed.

Christmas Eve at the Bottom of the Sea

We lay in the English Channel at a depth of 25 metres. All was peace, except for the monotonous hum of the gyro-compass. The cook had brewed a punch—a Christmas punch : but it did not produce the right atmosphere. What was the cause ? The depths of the ocean, the absence of relatives, or was the spirit too weak ? We hurriedly added a bottle of Three-Star brandy, and the atmosphere grew more Christmaslike. Every one of the crew had received a marvellous parcel from the Women's Association at Nuremburg. I began to unpack mine at once. First appeared a small paper Christmas tree, which we put on a table, set with candles and lit up. This increased the feeling of festivity. Soon in front of every man lay a pile of stockings, socks, ear-protectors, mittens, shirts, fancy boxes of cigars, and sweets of every kind. A gramophone played " Still night, holy night," and each of us for a time imagined himself at home among his loved ones, not at the bottom of the sea. We kept it up until one in the morning, and then crept one after another into our bunks or hammocks, and silence reigned once more.

The following days brought storms and rough seas. One night was especially tragic. The waves were dashing savagely against the hull and we had to drop to half speed. I was on the engine-room watch when a heavy sea swept over the boat and a flood of water streamed through the ventilator into the oil-engine room. The sudden thinning of the air was observable in a strange feeling of oppression at the ears and the appearance of a salty deposit on the hot cylinder cases.

Suddenly the cry rang out : " Man overboard."

A sea that was moving faster than the boat had burst upon the deck from aft and swept overboard Able Seaman No. 2. The helmsman at once threw him a lifebelt, but at the same moment an enemy destroyer appeared and we had to dive.

The raging sea had taken its first victim.

NEW YEAR, 1915

The wind was icy cold : the moon emerged fitfully from behind the driving clouds. The look-out men, chilled and stiff, stood at their posts.

Smoke-clouds on the port bow !

" Smoke-clouds on the port bow ! Looks like an enemy."

At this, the Commandant, Captain-Lieutenant Schneider, hurried up. He was aware that what he saw was an English squadron. Ghostlike in the moonlight the line of battleships moved along the far horizon.

" Full speed ahead ! "

" Diving-stations ! "

I rushed to the control-room, leaving the oil-engine in charge of my friend Romulus. The entire crew were tense with excitement, and in the minds of one and all was the single thought : " If only we can get at the English ! "

With set faces and taut muscles everyone—officers and men—stood at their action-stations. All knew what was expected of them.

The sea was too rough to keep the boat at periscope-depth. We pitched up and down at a varying depth of between 10 and 16 metres, which greatly added to the Commander's difficulties. When the Chief Engineer reported that he could not keep the ship at periscope-depth, the Commander decided to come to the surface.

Speechless, we stared at each other. We were in for it now ! Both the motors were working at full pressure ; the steel hull quivered as the boat shook off the mountainous waves that raced along the deck.

All we thought of was to get at the enemy.

There were now hardly 100 metres between us and the ship ; a few minutes and :

" Fire the port torpedo."

A shock, and the torpedo sped on its appointed way.

" Dive."

A frightful crash. " Hit ! "

H.M.S. *Formidable* heeled over. In wild excitement one of the sailors pulled out the gramophone and was about to turn it on ; but the hour for that had not yet come.

We soon came up to the surface again, and started chasing another ship ; but this one moved so fast that we could not catch up with her. We turned back again to our already wounded victim, with a view to giving her the death-blow. We had been moving under water for an hour before it was possible to make the second attack.

Scarcely had the torpedo left the tube, scarcely had we dived a few metres deeper, than there was a terrific burst of firing from the English battleship, and a frightful crash against our vessel suddenly put all lights out ; the boat listed over to port and plunged downwards until it lay on the sea-bottom at a depth of 47 metres.

The Commander soon appeared in the control-room and told us that we had got too near the English ship before firing the torpedo : he had not been able to turn and had to pass under the sinking ship, and we had apparently fouled her hull.

The boat was now examined ; no damage was found. The deep-sea watch was set, and we celebrated the New Year in a glass of punch which the cook made rather stronger this time, and in gossip about our late success.

Suddenly the stoker came in and reported that he had heard a suspicious knocking against the hull. Investigation revealed nothing, but a frightful clatter outside soon alarmed us all, and Able Seaman No. 1 expressed the view that a diver was drawing a net across us. The noise came nearer and nearer, and it really sounded as though a diver in his lead shoes were shuffling across the deck. When the man went on to suggest that the diver was drilling through our compressed-steel hull, I said : "Karl, fetch me a heavy hammer; I'll make that drill look silly when it comes through." They all laughed, and our alarm vanished. As we were lying on the sea-floor and there was a heavy ground swell, stones were rolling and clattering over our deck. They it was that had so startled us.

Next morning we rose to the surface. When we tried to raise the periscopes we found they would not work. So we had to come up. The conning-tower hatchway also refused to open, as the two periscopes had been bent at right angles across the top of it. Some of us hurriedly climbed on deck through the crew's hatchway ; the two periscopes were straightened and the conning-tower hatch raised. Fresh air streamed in.

Comforting ourselves with the thought that we were still alive, we started our return journey.

Admiral Schröder received us at Zeebrugge and congratulated us on our success.

4

U-BOAT CO-OPERATION

By

Commander Karl Neureuther, Commander of UB 73

A LIGHT haze hung over the North Channel, the northern entrance to the Irish Sea. The sun shone gratefully through the white air on to the conning-tower, where five sturdy U-Boat sailors were enjoying the warmth.

There was enough visibility to allow us to stay on the surface, but we had to keep pretty wideawake, for we could not see further than three to four miles. At that distance the sea melted into a white haze, though the sky above us was a deep and shining blue.

Both Diesel engines were going at half-speed, and we altered course every three minutes to protect ourselves against attack by enemy U-Boats.

The enemy was not as yet much in evidence. In the early morning a large convoy had passed us, but unfortunately at so great a distance as to give us no chance of attacking them. Our U-Boat was now moving eastwards towards the narrower entrance to the Channel in the hopes of finding richer prey and better opportunities of attack.

A note was handed up to the Commander from below. " Wireless from U 53. Enemy convoy on square x—y steering E.N.E.," with a comment from the operator, " U 53 must be quite near."

Shortly afterwards, indeed, the German U-Boat U 53 came into sight, making north-east : a few minutes later the boats were within hail, and exchanged news. While our boat, UB 73, was outward bound and intending that day to make the Irish Sea through the North Channel, U 53—Captain-Lieutenant Rose—was on her way home ; she had fired every torpedo but one, and could look back on a mass of tonnage sunk. He could, in general, only report that there was "plenty doing" in the Irish Sea. We were very ready to believe this, and, keen as we all were, the boats felt a touch of silent envy—they of our prospects and we of their success. U 53 told us that they had seen the convoy in question very shortly before, but then lost sight of it, and had not been able to attack it, mainly because, owing to the thick weather, they could not get close enough ; added to which, owing to defective air-leads, they could not blow two of their tanks, and hence could not dive quickly.

Meanwhile the two boats were moving in a westerly direction side by side. But they gradually drew apart, and the conversation had to be continued, no longer by megaphone, but by semaphore " Commander to Commander."

Suddenly our talk was broken into by a signal from U 53, which was leading : " Enemy in sight on starboard bow." Followed by : " Commander to Commander. Suggest combined artillery attack " ; our reply to which was, naturally : " Agreed " ; and the gun's crew appeared forthwith on deck. We seemed in for an eventful day, for behind the enemy ship, a steam trawler, there were signs of something very promising. Soon after came a signal from U 53 : " Port bow, cruiser and convoy in sight."

There she was ! A large old cruiser at the head of a convoy, as yet very faintly defined, but clearly recognisable as such.

Soon after a further signal from U 53 : " Commander to Commander ; am attacking " ; the alarm-bells rang, the conning-tower hatch slammed behind the Commander, and in a few minutes our boat was diving at full speed to the proper depth for attack, while U 53, remaining on the surface, altered course and was soon out of sight.

The boats were within hail.

Slowly the convoy came nearer—about twenty fine well-laden steamers. It was escorted by several destroyers in addition to the cruiser. The Commander issued his orders calmly and confidently : everyone was conscious of the gravity of the moment.

While we were manœuvring into position to attack two large steamers which had dropped slightly out of the centre of the line towards the left wing, we observed with joy that an enemy destroyer which had been darting about in most unpleasant proximity to us had turned at full speed towards the south. And it really looked as if another were on the point of following her.

Ah, wasn't that a depth charge? And another! And a third! The noise of the explosion was quite audible, but far away. Three cheers for our valiant comrades and friends of U 53. With equal astuteness and audacity they had stayed so long on the surface that all the destroyers had gone in pursuit of her.

We, therefore, were able to proceed with our task at leisure and undisturbed. The great steamers were bearing directly down upon us : we turned slowly to prepare to fire two bow torpedoes simultaneously at the two largest ships within range. One was about 400 metres away, and the other 800 metres. Unfortunately, it was very calm, so that the enemy would probably see the track of the torpedoes, which would be very soon and clearly visible, so we drew a little closer and fired at about 300 and 700 metres respectively.

A large burst of smoke shot up into the sunshine under the first steamer's bridge, while the second torpedo sped on its way to the second and more distant victim. But, alas, the track of the torpedo was too clearly visible. It was observed by the second steamer, which turned, and we waited in vain for the crash of the second explosion. It was fate, with which the U-Boat Commander must reckon for a long while until, by the favour of Heaven, a torpedo is invented that is not driven by compressed air, and leaves no track of discharged air behind it.

But our chief gratitude was due to our comrades of U 53, who did not allow their boat's defective diving capacity to prevent them diverting the escort's attention, and thus enabling us to attack, as far as possible, safe and undisturbed.

Unfortunately, such opportunities for generous co-operation towards a common success were rare : our U-Boats were so few in number that it was seldom possible to arrange it. But an unexpected meeting was always a happy chance ; and it was a still happier chance when—as in this instance—at the exact moment of meeting a convoy appeared on the scene and offered both boats the opportunity of such victorious common action.

5

CAPTAIN " SWIVEL-EYE "

By

Boatswain's Mate Christof Lassen

THE weather had been growing daily worse : huge seas came racing down upon our stern, and the after part of the boat was continually deep under water. The hellish howling and roaring of the sea was dreadful and sinister, and it was impossible to stay on deck without being lashed to one's place.

That day, however, the weather cleared a little. We all hurried on deck and made ourselves comfortable as soon as we could. How delicious it was to draw deep breaths of the fresh salt air ! Later on the sea grew calmer still, and soon it lay before us as smooth as a mirror.

A shout from the conning-tower : " Smoke-cloud, two points to starboard."

The Commander ordered the " Alarm " to be rung, and the sunshine and pure air soon vanished. I was at the horizontal rudder wheel with my eyes fixed on the depth-gauge.

The two bow torpedo-tubes were ready for action.

Then the Commander's voice rings out : " Steamer approaching, about 4,000 tons." Shortly after came the expected crash, and we came up at once and made towards the steamer's lifeboats.

A tall, broad-shouldered Scot came on board and introduced himself as the captain. He asked if he might bring his first officer with him, so that he could break his head for not reporting our periscope in time. He brandished his arms in the air ; his words poured in a torrent from his great mouth, and his eyes rolled horribly. Our cook christened him "Swivel-Eye."

The Commander, with an amused smile, refused our friend Swivel-Eye's—for so we called him from that moment—request; he grumblingly gave way, and in half an hour he was telling us he would like to be naturalised in Germany.

"Yes; in Ruhleben," retorted the Commander.

Swivel-Eye took charge of the other "guests" who were already domiciled on our boat, and they willingly obeyed him. He decided when each of them should go on deck, and when the alarm-bell rang he roared out "Diving-stations!" and he often kept me company at the horizontal rudder wheel. At night Swivel-Eye slept in the Petty Officers' cabin, under the table, which was occupied by the leader of the gun-crew.

This idyll was painfully destroyed one night. The wind was freshening to a gale, and the boat was pitching and rolling furiously. Suddenly—at the impact of an unusually heavy wave, no doubt—everything that was not positively clamped to its place crashed about the cabin in confusion, and the gun's crew leader fell on to Swivel-Eye's stomach. The latter at once struck a defensive attitude, thinking his last hour had come; there was a copious flood of German and English expletives, and a free fight, until Swivel-Eye realised what had happened and recovered himself. They finally agreed that this time they would both tie themselves to the table. No cordage was available, so they each sacrificed their braces, and with a friendly "Good-night" the usual snores began again.

Next morning, at breakfast, as we were laughing over the surprising events of the night, the alarm-bell rang.

We hurried to our stations. Swivel-Eye rushed into the Petty Officers' cabin, where his little flock were breakfasting, and bundled them with his great fists to their diving-stations. He himself sat down quietly with the cook, with whom he had struck up a prudent friendship.

The boat was soon under water: all was quiet in the conning-tower, and not a word was heard from above.

At last came the order : " First and second tubes ready ! "

We gradually learned that an unobtrusive-looking tramp steamer under the Norwegian flag had strayed into our range. The second officer of the watch, who had inspected the apparently harmless steamer through his periscope, suggested that we should come up to the surface and deal with it at leisure.

But the Commander did not care to risk this.

The tubes were reported ready.

" First tube, stand by ! "   Deadly silence reigned.

" Fire ! "

We let her go at 15 metres depth.   Only a few seconds' breathless silence, then a terrific crash.

" Hit ! "

In the same instant, the port bulwarks on the steamer fell forward and revealed . . . four guns, with their crews lying beside them.   A U-Boat decoy !

" Swine ! " rapped out the Commander and gave her a second torpedo at once.   A frightful detonation announced another hit.   The force of the explosion was such that our boat was flung several metres forward.   We stared at each other in horror.   Swivel-Eye wanted to climb up the conning-tower and jump off the boat ; he thought we had struck a mine. But soon came a shout from the Commander :   " U-Boat decoy sunk ! "

There had been some forty depth charges on the ship's after deck, and it was the explosion of these that had given us such a shock.

A few minutes later we came up to the surface to view a dreadful scene of destruction.   Three only of the crew had survived and were rowing towards us in a shattered lifeboat. Swivel-Eye took them under his wing and appointed them potato-parers to the Commander and cleaners of the fo'castle ; and I observed on several occasions that the standard of cleanliness was remarkably high.

All was going smoothly once more.   Our " guests " had now

reached the total of nine.   Slowly we turned and set our course for home waters.

It was Maundy-Thursday when a huge 7,000-ton steamer was sighted about nine in the forenoon, followed at a short distance by a smaller one under the Norwegian flag.   The Commander aimed at the large ship and torpedoed her ; but she seemed to have a charmed life and was still afloat after the second torpedo.   Meantime the small Norwegian had taken her crew on board and steamed off.   We came up to the surface to shoot a few holes in the obstinate creature's hull, when suddenly our starboard Diesel engine gave out.   At the same moment, 200 metres to port, a periscope emerged from the water and bore straight down on us.   To turn the wheel hard a-port and set the engines at full speed was the work of an instant ; but the Englishman was nearly on us.   Our gun was useless, as we should have damaged our own stern by firing at so short a distance.   Then the Englishman fired four torpedoes—two starboard and two port—at point blank range.

" Missed, thank God ! "

We had been lucky once again.   If the port instead of the starboard engine had failed, we should have had to turn in a wider circle, and the British torpedoes must inevitably have hit us.

" One 7,000-ton steamer and four torpedoes," observed the Commander cheerfully, " is not such bad work for a Maundy-Thursday."

We came to the surface towards evening and made for home.

At Wilhelmshaven, alongside our supply-ship *Hamburg*, Swivel-Eye assembled his little company on deck, and, after a short speech, called for three cheers : one for the Commander, one for the officers, and one for the crew.   Then he said good-bye to everyone personally and set forth on his way to the prison-camp at Ruhleben.

6

ENGINE REPAIRS AT SEA

By
Engine-room Artificer Nikolaus Jaud

FOR three days we had been cruising through the North Sea in all directions without sighting a single enemy ship. Our Commander, Captain-Lieutenant Remy, then set a course for the Orkneys to see what he could do in English waters. We were not far distant from these islands when the port Diesel engine failed. A small-end bearing had cracked. Such a thing had not happened since 1913—for the U 24 had been in service as long as that. Before we put to sea both oil-engines had been newly lined up, and here we were, only a few days later, in trouble already. The port engine was at once carefully examined, the oil-tank cleaned, and the crankcase washed with lubricating oil to make sure that there were no tiny fragments of metal remaining that might cause fresh disturbance. But this did not meet our chief trouble. Among our spare parts we had no small-end bearings.

The Commander swore, and the Chief Engineer and everyone in the engine-room pulled long faces. What were we to do? Go back? Or go on with defective engines?

"Go back? No!" said the Commander in a tone of stern resolve. He had had bad luck on his last voyage, having come back with only 50 per cent. of hits. What that means only those can know who have had Florian Geyer as Chief of their flotilla. If we came back now we need not expect to be welcomed with a band, or received personally by the Chief. Going back was out of the question. So I decided to cast a new bearing, and Chief Engineer Braun agreed.

ENGINE REPAIRS AT SEA

While the chief mechanic shook his head doubtfully, I made the necessary preparations with my friend Grube, an oil-room stoker. To attempt to cast a spare part on the high seas with completely inadequate instruments was certainly a bold undertaking.

To begin with, an exact tin copy of the bearing was constructed on the vice in the E. room and fitted to the small-end bolts. Upon this we made a mould of bread and asbestos packing, so that the metal should not run. A small anvil and a container were made out of a floor plate and the wooden grating in the E. room was cut up for firewood. We had no bellows; but for this the compressed-air installation could be made to serve.

Now we could get on : it was to be hoped that we should not be disturbed.

Black thick smoke poured out of the hatchway. The melted metal, consisting of a piece chipped off a spare main bearing, trickled into the container, which had first been carefully warmed with a soldering lamp. All the lads stood open-mouthed round the container, as though some magic potion were being brewed. The metal soon became liquid. Even the starboard engine had to be left to its own devices for a few minutes, for every member of the crew wanted to be present at the fateful moment. . . . All was well ! The metal flowed clean and clear into the improvised mould.

The fire was quickly taken out of the compartment, which was well ventilated, and the E. room hatch was closed. While the casting was getting cool my assistants and I swallowed a hurried meal, which we were not to have an opportunity of doing during the next twenty-four hours.

When I broke the mould about an hour later and the new bearing emerged without any flaws or porous patches I was hugely delighted. Darkness now had fallen, and I could quietly and without fear of disturbance file the bearing down to $\frac{1}{10}$ mm. and smooth away the grooves made by the asbestos thread. In the meantime the port engine was dismantled, and the piston, which weighed more than 2 cwt., and the connecting rod taken out. Eager willing hands succeeded in putting the engine together again by the next morning.

" Port engine in working order," I reported to the Commander, who warmly congratulated me.

We were now proceeding full speed ahead to the west coast of England. We all breathed more freely and awaited what might happen. And what did happen? A further engine defect was reported—actually a second small-end bearing had given way. It was now clear that the dockyard was at the bottom of this ill-luck. Either the metal used had been overheated, or some destructive element had got into it. However, no grumbling or abuse would help us out of our quandary. Once more I set up my casting apparatus, once more I had to spend twenty-four hours in the hot, steamy oil-room . . . and once more I succeeded. But by this time I was about fed up with it, and felt as though I could sleep for days.

I had been dead asleep for five hours when a stoker shook me. " What's the matter ? "

" You must come and see to the engine at once."

With gloomy forebodings I made my way aft.

" Another damned bearing gone ! Dockyard work again ! "

I repeated the manœuvre for the third time. Practice makes perfect. The engine was in working order again in twelve hours.

But now I really had to rest, and I was soon in my bunk. Once more I was awakened. I sprang up in a dazed condition and yelled at the First Lieutenant who stood beside me : " What's the matter now ? "

" We've just sunk a large sailing-ship with a cargo of corn, my lad."

And I knew nothing about it ! I must, indeed, have slept well. I went along to the engine, examined it thoroughly and found everything in excellent order.

" Next time we sink a steamer," said the Chief Engineer, " you go on board and get some bearing metal. We don't

need a dockyard any more, now we've got our own foundry."
And he laughed heartily.

We had soon reached the southernmost point of England,
which was to be our scene of operations. Here, a year and a
half ago, we sank an English steamer whose captain we had
greatly admired. A 6,000-ton steamer flying the Norwegian
flag passed ahead of us. We fired a shot across her bows and

Our torpedo plunged into the enemy's ribs.

she stopped. Cautiously we approached, but there was life
in her yet ; she tried to ram us. However, our Commander
had been on his guard. A general chase began. Suddenly
the Navigating Officer grabbed at the signal-pistol and shot
a white flare on to the enemy's bridge. The captain started
back, and in the self-same moment our torpedo plunged into
the enemy's ribs. He could ram us no more ; the steamer lay
quiet, rising and falling on the long rollers. From the after
hold rose a volume of thick yellow smoke, no doubt from

a cargo of sulphur. The crew got into the lifeboats and sailed away. Only the captain stayed behind, running up and down like a man possessed, crying that he would sink his own ship. We offered to take him off in our lifeboat, but he refused to come. Then, as smoke clouds became visible on the horizon, we fired some shells into the stern of the ship to sink her. The captain leaped off the bridge, worked his way to the stern, which was settling into the water, pulled down the Norwegian flag, hoisted the Union Jack, and went down with his ship. We stood on deck and watched the heroic death of a brave English sailor.

Our engines were working well and we proceeded on our course into the Irish Sea. We were soon in pursuit of an 8,000-ton steamer which, after a series of futile zig-zags, hoisted a white flag. The crew hurriedly left the ship and our Commander fired twelve rounds into her hull. But the Navigating Engineer reminded the Commander that we needed bearing metal.

" Why, of course ! Cease fire and get out the dinghy."

The Assistant Navigating Officer, two seamen and I rowed across to the steamer.

Karl, our torpedo gunner's mate, shouted after me : " If you can find a lathe, we shall get on with our repairs even quicker."

We clambered up the Jacob's ladder, looked back at our U-Boat, and saw it dive at that very instant. There we were, alone on a sinking ship ; not at all a pleasant feeling. If the English caught us we might very well be hanged as pirates. The officer and a seaman went up on to the bridge, the other seaman waited in the dinghy, and I made my way down into the engine-room to get some bearing material. But I was met by a swirl of water and hurriedly had to retrace my steps. I ran on to the deck and found myself confronted by a table laid for a meal. I swung round quickly, for I did not know what to lay my hands on first. Then I saw an open door ; I rushed in. The right place at last. Shelves packed with bottles and preserves, and against the wall hung a row of magnificent hams. Having stuffed my clothes-bag (which I had brought with me) with these precious articles, I ran out and fell over a hundredweight sack of coffee. " I must take this too," thought I, slung it over my shoulder and panted towards the ladder. A length of piping tripped me up, the coffee-sack burst, and the beans rolled and rattled down the sloping deck into the water.

The man in the dinghy shouted " She's sinking ! "

Not a moment was to be lost. I grabbed at a valise that was standing near the rail and stumbled down into the boat.

Scarcely had we rowed a few strokes from the steamer than, with much groaning and crashing, she went down. Ten seconds earlier, and we should have kept the coffee-beans company.

Meantime the U-Boat had come up and received us and our possessions. But we were to come upon some further treasures. Various casks and crates were seen to be floating on the surface of the water ; more and more appeared, and finally the sea all round us was strewn with them. The pressure of water had burst the sunk steamer's holds, and the cargo was coming to the surface.

One of the crates was soon fished out of the water and its contents examined. We could hardly trust our eyes ; it was pure American hog's lard. Everyone of us wanted to call such a crate his own, and we were all after them. In the literal sense of the word, we swam in fat. A derelict lifeboat had also emerged and lay rocking gently among the crates. Two ratings promptly jumped into it and disappeared. The boat had no bottom. Roars of laughter greeted the reappearance of the two " seals."

The deck of the U-Boat became gradually piled with crates, so that the Commander was forced to put an end to that fishing. But the two " seals " had not yet returned. After their unwelcome bath in the bottomless boat they had gone on fishing for crates and had drifted 500 metres away from us. They had two enormous crates in tow. When they were got on board they were, of course, immediately opened ; one contained twelve half carcases of pigs, and the other—dungforks.

We sacrificed the tridents to the god Neptune, who would no doubt make good use of them, but the pork we stowed away below. We were now well off for supplies and could pursue our voyage in comfort. The pork was boiled over an electric stove, and the lard was melted. The cook found himself in continual difficulties, as the stokers carried all the saucepans aft. We all positively shone with fat, and from that time onwards our leather overalls were really waterproof.

A couple more enemy steamers were sent to the bottom in the course of the next few days, and then we went home.

When we got back to Wilhelmshaven our Commander was able to report 100 per cent. of hits, and I could congratulate myself on having contributed to the success of the voyage.

7

BAVARIANS IN THE IRISH SEA

By

Chief Petty-Officer Roman Bader

THE look-out man I was relieving told me the usual story about the position of the boat, its present speed and direction, which, so far as I did not know them from the map, I had already found out on my way through the control-room. He then left me with good wishes for my spell of duty and I wished him a good sleep.

Now we were alone in that vast silence. By we, I mean my countryman Hans and myself, two solid Bavarians, on the conning-tower of a U-Boat, which, in the middle of February, 1917, was on the watch for victims in the Irish Sea.

It was four o'clock in the morning. Neptune was apparently asleep, for the sea was calm, or else he was stirring the salt soup with his trident somewhere else. Æolus, too, had laid his harp aside. The only wind was the faint breeze caused by the movement of the boat. With soothing regularity our M.A.N. Diesel hammered out its sturdy song of toil, and under the guidance of our third countryman Joseph, who steered with truly royal Bavarian calm, the graceful boat slid through the sea as though it ran on rails.

" Good morning, Hans," said I, forgetting my navy manners, in broad Bavarian to Hans, and he promptly answered in the same dialect. He had been born and bred at the foot of the highest Bavarian Alpine peak, where I, a native of Munich, had spent a large part of my youth in the house of my grandparents.

" Splendid weather, Hans."

" Not so bad."

" Any English about, do you think ? "

" What's Seppl doing ? "

" What should he be doing ?   Steering, of course."

Seppl, who was at the wheel below, was a man from the forests, a sturdy, willing youth with the innocent habit, when excited, of addressing me, his superior in rank, as " *Old boy*—I mean, Sir."   There we were, the three of us, an Alpine detachment at sea under one of the best-known and most successful Commanders of the Flanders U-Boat Flotilla, who had been awarded the *Pour le Mérite* for his achievements.   We three Bavarians were determined to do as well as all our comrades who had been born within sound of the sea ; indeed, we aspired, if it might be, to do even better than they.

Our native qualities had given us certain aptitudes for our duties on the U-Boat.   Hans, who had brought down many a bird and beast on the mountains of his home, was leader of the 8·8 cm. gun crew, and his sharp eyes had sent many an English ship to the bottom.   Seppl, with his iron nerves, distinguished himself at the wheel ; and I myself, who had done much sailing as a hobby, found myself in charge of the look-out men—in naval language, Number One—added to which I also functioned as a sniper and took turns with our Navigating Officer in blowing up captured ships.

Hans and I stood back to back, each turning in a half-circle on our own axis, from starboard to port and back again, sweeping the sea with our powerful Zeiss binoculars.   If the glasses became clouded we polished them with pieces of chamois leather that were dried over the electric light in the conning-tower.

" It couldn't be calmer on Starnberg Lake," said Hans suddenly.   " And there's often a cloud on the southern shore of the Ammer Lake like that one to port."

" That's so," I agreed, and made a mental leap from the Hamburg waterside, where I knew my brave, anxious wife was waiting, to the lovely land of Bavaria.

" But I hate that milk-soup over there," I added, meaning the mist. " One can't see properly, and it makes excellent cover for the enemy."

" I believe you," answered Hans. " Still, you don't exactly expect the English to bring you flowers on your birthday, do you ? You'll have to be satisfied with my good wishes." And he shook me warmly by the hand.

I was very glad that someone beside myself had remembered my birthday on this perilous voyage. Shortly after, the man at the wheel was relieved. A head appeared over the edge of the conning-tower hatch and asked whether he could come and take the air. Permission being given, the entire body emerged from the interior of the vessel, and even before Seppl— for it was he—had filled his huge lungs with the fresh morning air, he clicked his heels together, stood like a pagoda in his leather overalls, and, nodding with his excitement, blurted out : " Congratulations, Old boy—I mean, Sir."

" God reward you ! "

We laughed and shook hands, and as it was now growing lighter, and to strike a match no longer meant a risk of being seen, we lit up in celebration of the day, and made a list of contributions that we should exact from the enemy for my birthday dinner.

A light rising breeze lifted the mist, revealed the coast, and blew the haze in tatters out to sea. With straining eyes we searched the surrounding waters. At last, when Seppl was just about to go below to get some sleep, one of the strips of mist darkened slightly. This suspicious change of colour did not, of course, escape our practised eyes. Smoke? For a few seconds we peered at it intently, and were then certain that this dark fleck was a smoke-cloud. When the outline of the ship was discernible, Seppl went below and reported to the Commander, " Ship on port bow," and I changed course towards the tiny black smear. In the meantime the mist had been blown upwards and was slowly concentrating into clouds moving gently towards the English coast.

When the Commander appeared on deck—that is to say, on the conning-tower—the steamer was already so clearly visible that the alarm signal had to be given at once, and we dived so as not to be sighted too soon.

The enemy ship, a shabby old tub, typical of the coasting trader in the Irish Sea, steamed calm and unsuspecting to her destruction. She did not appear to be a U-Boat decoy ; she had no innocent-looking deck-wheelhouse that concealed a gun, no signal halyards between the masts that so often served as wireless antennæ, and she lay much too deep in the water to conceal any unpleasant surprises between decks. She was certainly directly helping to destroy Germany, and to carry on a system of war that thrust into the hands of innocent German children a slice of raw onion for their supper. We could not spare that ship, however much we might regret it.

When I travelled about on leave and so often saw children whose angel-souls shone through their pale starved bodies, or soldiers, themselves but skin and bone, carrying home their last loaf to their wives whose hour was nearly come, I was seized with fury against this inhuman enemy who had cut off Germany's food imports. And what I felt all my comrades on the sea felt too.

It was the enemy's crime that forced sailors like ourselves to sink floating palaces, masterpieces of human ingenuity and workmanship.

And so this freighter came within our grasp. The Commander valued the last torpedo far too highly to use it upon so unimportant a vessel. So we prepared for a fight on the surface. Shells with time or contact fuses, explosive charges, rifles, pistols and hand-grenades were got ready. The boat was soon ordered to the surface. The depth-gauges swung back, the water against the round conning-tower porthole soon glittere with the light of day, and an instant later we could hear it pouring off the hatch. A twist of the bolt, a heave, the hatch is open, and the Commander and I climbed on to the deck, which was now clear of water. Hans emerged from below with his range-finder, ran to the 8·8 cm. gun, and made ready for action. While we hoisted the flag on the conning-tower the rest of the crew hurried on deck.

" Heave-to at once ! " Before we had succeeded in getting the range, the enemy vessel, after a half-hearted attempt to turn away and escape, lay still. A lifeboat was lowered, and we observed that other boats were being manned and launched. The first boat rowed towards us. A flag had been hoisted— the ship was English. The captain duly handed over his ship's papers, introduced himself as an Englishman, and at once asked what we proposed to do with his ship, himself, and his crew. He blurted out all this in a way that contrasted rather noticeably with his stolid appearance and movements. I did not altogether like the look of him, and while the Commander was talking to him I had my hand on the butt of my Dreyse pistol ; nor did I take my eyes off this singular visitor. He was a thorough Englishman, a trader through and through, a brutal egoist laboriously concealing his terror. The Commander and I were just about to answer the man's questions, when I noticed the captain's cold grey eyes looking over my shoulder. A moment later the Lieutenant's sharp voice was heard shouting to the Commander : " Another ship in sight ! "

The Commander turned away to give fresh orders. I did not take my eyes off the Englishman, and told him that his fate depended on himself. "All right," he said savagely ; " then hurry up and sink the —— old tub and let me go. That's my friend Jack, and behind him are three more." And he gave me the names of the ships, the captains and the first officers, and he told me the cargo they were carrying and their port of destination. I was completely taken aback by the Englishman's candour. I at once reported this information to the Commander, and continued to keep this engaging gentleman company on the U-Boat deck. Meantime our Navigating Officer and his men had performed their appointed task of blowing up the ship.

In the course of our conversation I obtained some more

interesting facts from our new friend. His vessel and some others had collected in their port of departure to wait for an armed escort : they waited a long while, but the escort did not come, and, as their precious cargo of metal was much needed at their port of destination, and freightage, etc.—for it was all a question of money—was not being earned while they lay in harbour, the owner decided they had better take the risk and go without an escort ; and so, in order not to attract attention, they put out to sea one by one, with a considerable interval between each departure.

"Yes, Sir," he went on, with copious expletives, "we were to start that night and it was settled I should go first. I was blind when we sailed. Well, Sir, I know my way about this bloody pond, so I said we should go full speed across the open water and then keep along the banks ; you know where I mean, all the way from Tuskar to the Blackwater. All went well, we stoked all night and got the net over the funnel, so that there shouldn't be any smoke to give us away, and we fixed the ventilator so it couldn't open. The engineer got up full steam, and the old tub was fairly shaking with it. We managed to get along with hardly any smoke, when the fog came up. I had everything opened up again because I hadn't too much fuel. It didn't matter about the engine smoking in a fog. I was dead sure I would pull it off. Yes, Sir, I just took a drop of something that never does you any harm, and I was just going to lie down when you came along. So I thought to myself : ' If you're in for it, the others had better be in for it too.' If I alone come back without a ship I shall be taken for a fool, and I shan't get another command. I've got a wife and child, old boy, and I have to look ahead a bit. I'm not a fool. I said to myself : ' Fritz must get all four of them and not only me. Then none of us will get into trouble, the Government will pay up, and we shall all get ships again.' "

I caught a glint of fear in those hard eyes. He did not yet know what was going to be done with him. " Marvellous fellow," thought I.

Our " explosive party " came back, and the captain was allowed to row ashore in his own boat.

A crash and a roar. The Englishman saw the shattered fragments of his steamer sink below the surface. But we were tearing along at full speed towards our next victim. When the second ship sighted us, she turned away at once, but stopped equally abruptly when she saw her own signal flags floating from our improvised mast—the periscope. For, as we knew her name, it had been possible to deduce this from Lloyd's Register. Our own flag had twisted round the mast and was not recognisable, so the English captain took us for a British boat. He was plainly most surprised when he caught sight of the flag of the German Imperial Navy. We had come up nearly alongside, and gave the crew a little time to stow their personal possessions in the boats while we received the ship's papers from the captain. Meantime I and one of our men rowed across to the ship to blow it up. I put the appropriate charges under the engine plate and against the side of the hull beneath the water-line, while my companion kept a look-out above from the chart-house. As he reported nothing suspicious, I turned over the maps and diagrams on the table, drank a morning cup of coffee which stood there untouched, and saved a few large fresh English loaves from a watery fate.

Our dream of a birthday cake had come true.

I clambered quickly up the mast and looked round me.

" By God, there's No. 3 ! " I shouted to my companion. " But now we must hurry." I slid down to the deck, and lit the fuse in the engine-room ; then we both grabbed a few things to take away, swung ourselves into the boat, and rowed back.

The English captain was sent off in the lifeboat to join his crew.

We got ready to dive, for visibility was now very good, and waited for the explosion and destruction of No. 2. Then we dropped to periscope-depth and set off in pursuit of our next victim.

There was no time to eat our birthday cake—the English loaf—for we were soon on the surface near steamer No. 3, whose captain stared at us completely dumbfounded. We hailed him, received his papers, interviewed him, sank his ship, and dismissed the crew in their lifeboats—all in very quick succession.

The masts of the fourth steamer were now rising above the horizon. For the fourth time we repeated our manœuvres. As she did not stop at the first challenge, she had to be brought up sharply by a shell across her bows. When the captain's boat was within hail, we greeted him by name and ordered him to come on board with his ship's papers. The boat came alongside ; the captain jumped on deck and said :

" I suppose you have sunk two or three ships in front of me, and they told you all about us ? Well, it doesn't matter ; I should have done the same. The last ship will soon be along, but there's an escort with her."

The Englishman had betrayed to us what we did not know— that a fifth steamer would fall to our vengeance. When this ship was sunk, the captain was allowed to row ashore with the crew, while we searched for the fifth member of the party. As we saw her growing gradually clearer on the horizon, we also detected in her course a long trail of smoke that came from a ship with several funnels.

Caution and expedition were indicated.

A shot across her bows, the English ship lowered her lifeboats, we fired a few time and contact shells into her, and she at once began to heel over. The English destroyer dashed up ; we dived, and left her in undisputed control of the surface of the Irish Sea.

8

HURRICANE

By

Leading Seaman W. Schlichting

ONCE more the round red disc of the morning sun rose above the far horizon and announced another fine day, such as we had been enjoying for weeks past on the open sea. We had grown quite fond of our " Bright Hans," as the North Sea is called in good times when the light waves ripple over it. But woe when Bright Hans awakes ! He rises up and roars and bellows like a murderous giant.

Wavelets of foam-crowned green water rustled over the U-Boat's foredeck. Suddenly, to the north-west, a dark cloud appeared and slowly mounted the sky. The heaving of the waves increased, the heavens darkened, and the wind was already whistling the song we knew so well. Bright Hans's back became more deeply bowed and great waves, more than a man's height, bore down upon us : they broke in angry bursts of foam against the conning-tower, and their crests beat against the casing and streamed over on to the look-out men behind it.

The fore and aft hatches had long since been closed, and no one dared set foot upon the upper deck : he would have been swept overboard and out of sight of his aghast companions before he had had time to utter a shout.

Blacker and more ominous, the clouds kept rolling up, and, though it was early afternoon, sea and sky were veiled in darkness.

" Force 9, the wind," says the officer of the watch. The

barometer is still falling. Time to relieve the watch. Complete with oilskin shirt, trousers, jacket and tarred cape, and a sou'wester on my head, I stand ready to seize a favourable moment to leap up from the control-station, through the conning-tower hatch, and so to my look-out post. My friend Hein is quite sure that my oilskins will not hold out for long ; but we shall see.

Now ! In a brief moment between two oncoming waves I

Great waves . . . bore down upon us.

am through the hatchway, saluted by friendly grunts from my descending comrades and by a shower of spray from a breaker that immediately burst over me. " Damnably cold," is my first sensation. I am now steady and staring into the distance that is growing ever blacker. The day is turning into night. Everywhere, in all the yawning hollows of the waters, roars the storm : it howls and rages in the air and over the sea, as though the spirits in the clouds were holding festival and the wind were fiddling frantic measures for that dreadful dance.

" Force 12, the wind ! "

Our boat is caught in a hissing, swirling witches' cauldron. Each wave, as the seconds pass, seems to grow larger, and the last one looks ready to crash down upon us with even greater fury than its predecessor. Like bloodthirsty wolves with dripping jaws, watchful and cunning, they leap upon us from every side, and grind their teeth upon our vessel's walls, as she rolls and rocks and pitches. We have to clutch the conning-tower rail so as not to be washed overboard. Hissing hailstones rattle down upon us, and we vainly try to cover our faces and hands against this sting-ing artillery of heaven. Hein was right —my oil-skins begin to let the water through in places. And the cold is ghastly. Storm ! This is no longer a storm, but a raging, tearing hurri-cane. Crystal walls

No one ventured to set foot on the upper deck.

tower up before us, behind us, and on every side. Great sea-mountains rise out of the deep, crash down and nearly overwhelm us ; the boat creaks and groans in all her joints and rivets. Like a mad sea-monster, she leaps and wallows in the foaming flood. A dance of death.

Some years before, I had been seasick in a battleship in the High Sea Fleet ; and not I alone, but dozens of us. Cables were stretched across the deck so that no one should be washed overboard, and buckets were secured in convenient places in case there was not time to reach the railing. I had used those buckets, and I now thought myself immune. But that was nothing to what I was going through now ; what is a battle-ship in a storm compared to a U-Boat in a hurricane ? I could not struggle against the feeling of nausea that overcame me ; my stomach asserted its independence, and at last I made

Complete with oilskin shirt, trousers, jacket, and tarred cape.

my offering to Neptune, Ruler of the Sea, as I had done off Cape Skagen, but not, this time, in a bucket. The savage cold numbed my blood ; I was half frozen, and I never thought I should escape from this chaos. I was without hope and almost unconscious, and I should not have cared at all if the boat had been smashed to atoms.

But the longest watch comes to an end at last. My relief appeared, and I stumbled blindly down the hatchway and on to the officer of the watch, who was standing below and received my sea-boots in the middle of his back. I lurched along to my bunk. Here, too, in the forecastle, from the glistening green faces that met my eyes, Neptune seemed to have exacted his tribute. A pallid corpse-like countenance peered out at me from one of the bunks, and retched and retched. At this sight my own stomach began to turn again, and I could barely contain myself. The atmosphere below was really beyond description. The damp, warm, almost stifling air, saturated as it was with oil, made me feel sicker than ever.

Before I lay down I swallowed a little tea, and glanced into the engine-room ; an appalling burst of heat flung me backwards ; the thermometer stood at nearly 45° Celsius. The men were standing over their engines in the bare minimum of clothing, and their drawn, gaunt faces, smeared with oil and filth, looked like skulls. The air was unbelievable ; the thudding combustion-engines exhausted such fresh air as could be pumped through the ventilators, and what remained of it was not enough to lighten the prevailing atmosphere. Hot whirling eddies of vapour hovered over the engines and drifted to the other parts of the ship ; the men were continually mopping their foreheads, and now and again one of them would moisten his lips with a drop of repulsive lukewarm tea, which, like all the food and drink on the boat, tasted strongly of oil.

I fled from this steely oil-reeking domain and tried to get some sleep on my bunk. Though hitherto it had been the cold that made me curse my fate, it was now the foul air that made breathing a torture and would not let me sleep. Sweat broke from all my pores ; I tossed about and tried to wedge myself in every conceivable position so as not to be flung out by a sudden heave of the boat. Those five hours of rest, that were mere restlessness and torment, seemed eternal, and the summons to turn out again cmae almost as a relief. Exhausted and shattered, without a wink of sleep, I hoisted myself out of my bunk and went to my post in the control-room.

The storm was still raging and flung sheets of foaming water across the boat. Bright Hans was still hungry for his prey.

The look-out men were now going through what I had endured four hours before ; now and again I ventured a glance through the central periscope, though it was mostly obscured by streaming water.

One of the engineers, an old sailor, who had sailed the North Sea for years in a trawler, and had appeared indifferent to the weather, came into the control-room and began to yarn. The longer he went on, the more hair-raising became his stories of the storms he had been through, and the conclusion of his discourse seemed to be that our hurricane was a trifle. But when a petty-officer took occasion to mention that in his early days on a sailing-ship he had been through a blizzard off the American coast and a typhoon in the China seas, the other subsided and was ready to admit that such weather, with the wind at Force 12 and 55 to 60 metre-seconds of speed, was something more than a breeze. However, as no one would now listen to him, he fell more and more silent, and tried to take his revenge by sitting down to a dish of beans and bacon. His calculation was correct ; bacon, to my seasick belly, was like a red rag to a bull. He had got his own back.

Before my watch was at an end, the Commander appeared and ordered us to diving-stations ; he had decided to lie at the bottom until the weather, which was equally trying to the boat as well as the crew, should improve. A few minutes the boat was at rest on the sandy sea-floor about 35 metres beneath the surface. It was at last possible to get some sleep and collect a little strength into our weary bodies ; and my belly was greatly benefited by the rest. After some hours I was stirred from sleep by a few kindly blows in the ribs ; I awoke with a heavy head.

What sort of air was this ? It was not air at all ; it was a stifling haze of oil and grease that choked one's nose and throat. This was getting dangerous ; and so the Commander seemed to think, for in quick succession came the orders to get the boat up to the surface.

The storm had lost its violence ; a heavy rain was falling, and this had made the sea much calmer. It was my turn for the conning-tower watch, and very unpleasant this was in the steady rain. However, the sky soon cleared a little, and the sun seemed trying to break through. I watched with interest the conflict between sun and cloud, naturally hoping that the former would prevail. A purely selfish hope ; I wanted to be dry again and to be able to hang my clothes out on the deck. At the first ray of sunshine the men off duty crept out of their lairs. The dirty, shaggy faces peered from the hatchways and blinked in the sunshine ; indeed, it was some time before their eyes got used to the bright light. Very soon the steel hawsers over the conning-tower were hung with fluttering shirts and multifarious garments whose owners sat basking in the sun on deck.

9

TWICE RAMMED

By

Wireless Operator Kolland

OUR boat had been through all its tests, and we were to put to sea on the following day. The crew spent the last few hours of freedom in writing home. On the day of our departure we took a hurried bath, for there was no time nor opportunity for baths on a U-Boat. A few hours before we were actually due to start, we went on board to make sure that the engines and machinery were all in order. Some of the crew who had been visiting their friends now reappeared, and the last few hours and minutes quickly passed in lively conversation, grave and gay.

Silence fell when our Commander appeared, accompanied by the Admiral and a number of officers. The crew were piped up on deck, and, after a pithy discourse from the Admiral and three hearty cheers for Germany, the order was given to cast off. In an instant the cables were on shore, and the boat began to move slowly through the waterways of Pola harbour. The waving figures on the mole gradually diminished and disappeared. The Austrian destroyer which was to escort us through the mine-barrier was waiting, and guided us safely to the Cape Promontore lighthouse. After a last farewell to our Austrian comrades, and a polite exchange of flag-signals, we parted and set off at full speed on a zig-zag course to face an unknown destiny in the dangerous waters of the Adriatic.

Life on a U-Boat was a very close and intimate affair. We

were all interdependent ; " One for all, and all for one," was our unspoken watchword. Both when cruising and attacking, each man put his whole strength into the common purpose, and there was never a murmur of complaint at the hardships of the service. In success as in peril we knew that we were all working for the general good ; we were like a great family isolated on the wastes of ocean. We were a band of brothers, and there were no disputes or quarrels. I cannot conceive of a finer or more loyal community of life and labour than that of a U-Boat.

Our commission was to intercept the enemy's communications by sea along the routes to Marseilles and Genoa. Marseilles was the chief port for the supply of artillery, munitions, guns, arms of every sort, automobiles and foodstuffs, to the French Army. If we could succeed in dislocating this traffic, it would be an enormous relief to our comrades on the Western Front.

The weather was stormy ; waves dashed against the boat, and the task of the look-out men became increasingly difficult. Towards evening the sky cleared for a little, just long enough to allow them to catch a glimpse of several smoke-clouds. The alarm-bell rang for diving-stations.

When the Commander had marked down his victim—the largest steamer in the convoy—we started manœuvring for position. A hot chase began, and the constant change of course kept the chief helmsman very busy. The torpedo-room, too, was the scene of much activity ; the four torpedo-tubes were soon ready, and all stood waiting for the order to fire. In vain ! We had been chasing that steamer for more than an hour ; again and again, aided by the hazy weather, she had succeeded in eluding us. But our Commander was an obstinate man ; we held on, while the great vessel twisted and doubled like a hare. " Ah, I've got you now," the Commander would snarl ; and then : " Damn her, she's run into the mist again." The furious chase went on. At last, when we had been after her for nearly two hours, came the longed-for

orders : " First tube ready ; stand by . . . Fire ! " The
U-Boat quivered, and the torpedo sped from its tube.

" One . . . two . . . three . . . four . . ." Was it a
miss ? Then came the sharp crash of an explosion. " A
hit ! " But a sudden crash against our own boat stiffened us
in alarm. For a few seconds we stood helpless and paralysed
at our diving-stations. But the Commander did not lose his
head for an instant ; he rapped out the orders : " Full speed
ahead ; dive to 60 metres." We had collided with the sinking steamer. The deeper we dived, the more and more
water found its way into the fore part of the boat. We at once
started the pumps to get rid of as much of the invading water
as we could.

Such was our first mishap, but a second soon followed. The
patrol-vessels cruising above flung bomb after bomb at us, and
kept on our track with marvellous tenacity. After proceeding
under water for two and a half hours, we came up to the
surface with the proud consciousness of having crippled an
8,000-ton English steamer, and made a lucky escape from
imminent death. We collected on deck, and discovered that,
owing to the thick haze, the torpedo had been fired at a range
of only 60 metres ; and when we had, as usual, set the electric
motors at full speed ahead so as to swing round to port, we
had, at the very moment of turning, struck the steamer. The
U-Boat was so seriously damaged that we had to return
home.

A few weeks later the wild Atlantic waves were bursting over
our boat. This time our task was to intercept enemy ships on
their way to and from Africa. June 20th was to be a day of
both good and evil fortune. At 8.40 a.m. the look-out reported
the appearance of a convoy consisting of thirteen steamers and
seven patrol-boats, the latter being mostly destroyers and
trawlers. The alarm bell shrilled. We dived instantly,
altered course, and made for the convoy at full speed. After
manœuvring for an hour and a half, we got within about
600 metres of the line of ships and, as usual, chose the largest as

our victim. I went to my station aft to repeat orders from
above to the stern torpedo-room.

"First and second tubes ready!" This order did not
affect me, and I thought I should not be called on ; but I
was soon to be undeceived. Another order came down the
speaking-tube : "Third and fourth tubes ready!" I repeated
it to the men. And then, after a brief interval : "Prepare to
fire all four tubes!" We had complete confidence in our

We dived like lightning and made for the convoy.

Commander, but it seemed rather dangerous to attack with
all four torpedoes at the ready, especially as we could only
discharge two, or at most three, before we should have to dive
hurriedly. If by any chance the tube-door failed to close, the
pressure of water would probably explode the torpedo still
remaining in the tube. We were soon to know our fate ; a
few tense moments, and the order came : "First tube, stand
by!" The torpedo-gunner's mate stood at the speaking-tube
by the firing machinery in case anything went wrong in the
conning-tower, and a second man stood ready to close the
door when the torpedo had been fired. The order, "Fire!"

delivered us all from a paralysing nightmare : the boat shook and the torpedo sped on its way. A tremendous detonation announced the fate of the 2,000-tonner.

While we were still talking over this successful stroke the Commander had already manœuvred into position to attack the second largest steamer. The order " Stand by, second tube " had already been given, when the U-Boat suddenly listed at least 30 degrees to starboard. Every movable object crashed in confusion on to the floor.

" Dive to 50 metres," shouted the Commander. At that instant a depth-charge burst with a frightful explosion quite near the boat. The enemy was on to us. A deathly silence reigned below, and everyone waited for what might come ; we had no notion of what was happening above our heads.

When we reached a depth of 50 metres a leak was reported in the after compartment, caused by the rivets that had given way as the result of the depth-charge explosion, and the pumps were started immediately. The horizontal rudders were set for ascent, but, in spite of persistent activity at the pumps and the wheel, the boat continued to sink, and the depth-gauge recorded 70 metres. We laboured on in silence, occasionally glancing at the depth-gauge, which soon indicated 85 metres. Everyone was aware of the crisis. Our hopes grew fainter as the risk of being crushed by the pressure of the water or blown up by depth-charges increased. We worked on and on, if only to distract our minds from our imminent doom at the bottom of the sea. This voyage of death seemed like an eternity. The solemn stillness was broken only by the regular rhythm of the pumps. . . .

" Saved ! " No one dared to say it or believe it. But the boat slowly began to rise. The depth-gauge showed 70 . . . 60 . . . 50 . . . All might yet be well.

Alive and under the sky ! The clouds of smoke that had brought us so near to death were just vanishing behind us. We were amazed when we got on deck and had a look at the damage. The periscope was snapped right off, and the stays bent round the steel cables above the conning-tower. Just as our second torpedo was being fired, a patrol-boat sighted us, dashed at our periscope, and knocked the boat sideways. Thus, within a few weeks, we had been rammed twice. We at once did a few essential repairs and turned back to Pola.

After a successful six weeks' voyage, having sunk about 45,000 tons of shipping and fired twelve torpedoes, we entered Pola harbour safe and sound, escorted by an Austrian destroyer. There were many friends on the mole waiting to give us an uproarious welcome; and an answering cheer went up from all of us when the orderly appeared with the post that brought us greetings from our homes.

10

SIR ROGER CASEMENT'S LAST VOYAGE

By
Engine-room Artificer Karl Wiedemann

" WELL, do your best," said the Captain commanding the
Fourth U-Boat Flotilla, which had been guarding the Ems
estuary since the beginning of the war, to our Commander,
Captain-Lieutenant Weissbach. " Good luck ; and come back
safe."

We steered out of the harbour and set a course for Heligoland. Sky and sea were grey and colourless ; there was a
gentle swell in the North Sea. At Heligoland we found U 20
waiting for us ; as the result of a fractured horizontal rudder,
she had had to abandon her voyage and was now making
for home. But before leaving for Wilhelmshaven she was
required to hand over to us a dinghy and an out-board motor.
We sent a petty-officer out in the dinghy for a practice trip ;
when he had satisfied himself that it was serviceable and
seaworthy, the boat and the motor were stowed in our aft
torpedo-room.

In the meantime we had become much interested in a
Captain-Lieutenant and two petty-officers who were walking up
and down the mole. It was obvious that their uniforms did
not belong to them. We asked the crew of U 20 who these
men might be, but they had been forbidden to talk about
the three unknown, who shortly afterwards came aboard our
boat.

After a brief farewell to our comrades, we set out in north-
westerly direction accompanied by an escort of greedy sea-

gulls. The island of Heligoland dipped lower and lower into the sea until it soon quite disappeared.

Shortly afterwards the Commander assembled the crew on deck.

" On this occasion," he said, " we have a special duty to perform. We are not, for the moment, looking out for English ships. We have with us on board Sir Roger Casement, the leader of the Irish Nationalist Party, who is going to stir up his countrymen to revolt against England, and we are to land him on the Irish coast."

The secret of the three unknown men, who now appeared on deck in civilian clothes, was thus revealed. The oldest, who was distinguished from the others by a beard, introduced himself as Sir Roger, and described the other two as his trusty followers. Then he spoke to us of the difficult task that lay before him, and of the liberation of Ireland, and he added in a grave but confident tone : " The English Government has put twenty thousand pounds on my head ; here is an excellent opportunity to earn it."

Sir Roger was a pleasant man and soon became our friend. He talked to everyone on the boat, and showed a lively interest in our troubles and our country's peril. When he heard I came from Munich, his usually grave face lit up and he spoke with enthusiasm of my native city. Munich and the Lake of Starnberg had been his second home. " If the Germans had listened to me," he said suddenly, " and aimed at Dover-Calais instead of Paris, they would have beaten England and won the war."

A shout of " Diving-stations ! " broke off our conversation. Not an enemy in sight ; what could be the matter ? One of the port engine bearings had cracked, and we had to lie on the sea-floor while another was fitted. The damage was soon repaired and we were able to continue our voyage on the surface.

One evening Sir Roger appeared without a beard, and we knew that our destination was now not far away. We were near in-shore, and the boat had to be navigated with great care and caution.

" Diving-stations ! " shouted the Commander. Every man was at his post in an instant. The fore tanks were flooded, the electric engines were switched on, and the boat moved along on the surface with the conning-tower hatch open. For the last time, Sir Roger walked through the boat and shook hands with every member of the crew.

Two a.m. " Stop both engines ; all hands on deck," ordered the Commander. But the engine-room crew peered on to the deck and saw the dinghy put into the water. Sir Roger and his two companions got into the boat, followed by one of our men, who had soon rowed our guests ashore. The place was Tralee Bay.

Secretly, as we had come, we slipped away, leaving our late guest to his fate. The night was very dark and we were able to get out to the Atlantic unobserved. Once outside, we started hunting for enemy ships. We had already sent several to the bottom to keep Neptune company, when we were ordered to return. On our way home we torpedoed another English steamer, on which we found a recent English newspaper. To our horror we read that Sir Roger had already been taken and condemned to death for high treason. His execution took place three and a half months later, on August 6th, 1916.

11

OFF DUBLIN

By

Commander Karl Neureuther, Commander of UB 73

It was the night of April 15th-16th, 1918. Thick darkness hung over the Irish Sea. The look-out men on UB 73 anxiously scanned the smooth expanse of dark water.

" Can you still see her ? " says the Commander to the Navigating Officer.

" Yes, Sir, just a faint dark speck through my glasses."

Everyone turned and stared in the direction indicated until the Commander intervened : " Now then, my lads, you keep a good look-out astern and each side of us ; you aren't concerned with anything ahead."

The discipline of the watch was one of the fundamentals of U-Boat work ; and it was an important element in the exact adjustment of duties, without which such a weapon cannot achieve its purpose. In such a case, when the boat is moving at full speed, the Commander and the Navigating Officer control the navigation and keep a look-out ahead, while the other members of the watch have to keep a sharp look-out in other directions, a duty from which nothing should be allowed to distract them. Too often has it happened that when everyone is staring at the object of interest the U-Boat has been caught unawares.

" She seems to be turning to starboard, Sir."

" Starboard 10, course 345 degrees."

In a few moments comes a voice from the wheel : " Course 345 degrees."

The ship was now rather more clearly discernible. Her bow could be distinguished in the darkness by a white flicker of foam, and a little to the left there was a faintly defined darker fleck against the darkness of the night.

" Ask the Chief Engineer to come on deck," says the Commander, and in a few moments a figure in greasy overalls appeared and saluted.

" Can't you give us a bit more power, my dear Streng ? We've been after her for the last hour as hard as we can go, but she twists and dodges so that we can't get any nearer."

" With the best will in the world, Sir, I can't get another ounce out of her."

" Well, well ; then we must hope she'll do something foolish—run into a whale, perhaps."

The Chief Engineer, rather abashed by the fact that even the best of his kind cannot get more out of an engine than it is built to provide, disappeared down the hatchway.

To the watchers on the deck the boat seems to be going half a knot faster ; and yet it is only too certain that the wish is father to the thought. The distance between the U-Boat and that hunted shadow grows no less. The Warrant Officer follows it fixedly in his binoculars.

" She's turning to port."

" Port 10, course 345 degrees " ; and the helmsman repeats : " Course 345 degrees."

The steamer has swung sharply to the left ; the U-Boat turns still more widely so as to try to cut across her course. As the minutes pass, the watchers' eyes convince them that the distance has diminished. The steamer's outline is discernible— one funnel, two masts, and rather low deck-structures. She is probably a cargo-boat of not less than 6,000 tons.

Then follows a sharp succession of orders : " Second tube, stand by ; port 5, right. Diagonal bow shot to starboard ; angle 90 degrees." And the replies : " Course 305 degrees ; second tube ready ; angle 90 degrees."

The whole boat was alive with a self-enclosed existence. The motors were thundering at top speed and the boat was quivering in every plate. Each one of those thirty-odd heads in the crew was seething with excitement. At any moment the boat might slip within range and the tension be broken by the order " Fire ! "—when a torpedo would leap from the tube on its deadly journey. This momentous order is shouted through the whole boat, not for merely technical reasons ; the verbal repetition of it is intended to guard against the failure of the electric fire-direction in the conning-tower, but it is also a wise recognition of the fact that in this close community of battle every member of it ought to know when the decisive moment is at hand.

The boat, and the men within it, waited ; and every minute that expectation grew more tense and terrible. . . .

Slowly came the order from the conning-tower, and the ring of disappointment could be heard in the Commander's voice : " As you were with the second tube."

The steamer had again swung to starboard, and the distance between the two vessels was so great that it was useless to attempt a torpedo shot for the time being. There were many angry men on that U-Boat : the Commander ; the Navigating Officer, who could now barely see the great steamer as a faint black flicker in his binoculars ; the Chief Engineer, who could not make that extra half-knot ; and the torpedo gunner's mate, whose pride it would have been to say when he heard the dull crash of the detonation : " That's the stuff to give them." Perhaps, however, the angriest of all was a member of the crew who might be thought to have been least concerned—the cook. But on a U-Boat there is not a man who does not feel such a mishap as peculiarly his own. In short, every man of that crew was cursing as heartily as he knew how !

And so the chase went on, this way and that, behind the steamer shadow, and she gradually vanished out of our sight.

·The Navigating Officer lowered his binoculars, polished them with a piece of wash-leather, put them up again, and observed : " Can't see her now, Sir."

Meantime it had grown somewhat lighter ; a haze hung over the water, which the west wind had whipped into little white crests of foam ; it was the hour of falling twilight, when in such an atmosphere sea and sky are fused together and one moves through the world under a shade of milky glass.

" Trawler on port beam," said the port look-out man sharply, without moving an inch.

" Hard a-starboard," rapped out the Commander, and the boat circled away from the enemy in a sharp curve. The trawler was now clearly visible ; it did not change its course, and could not, therefore, have observed us. Then another trawler appeared, and, to the right of her, a third shadow was visible.

Sharp and quick came the orders : " Rudder midships ; hard a-port ; diving stations ; course 300 degrees."

The U-Boat swung in a narrow curve away from the fresh danger on a course exactly opposite to that of the approaching vessel. But it was too late. Even though the crew of the first trawler was afflicted with the proverbial somnolence of fisher-men, that of the second was quite wideawake. She immediately turned in pursuit of us. In a few seconds guns flashed from the first ship, and shells began to fall unpleasantly near. An artillery contest between a U-Boat with one gun and three trawlers with at least six guns in all offers little prospect of success. The wise man retires, and so, in this case, did the Commander of UB 73.

The alarm bell shrilled " Flood tanks ! "

Everyone on the conning-tower dashed down the hatchway, the Commander last of all. As he cast a final glance round the scene of action, he was a little startled to notice that there were now four trawlers in sight, all of whom had opened fire. In three-quarters of a minute the U-Boat had disappeared beneath the surface as the trawlers dashed up at full speed.

The U-Boat was now moving slowly on a course at right angles to that on which she had dived, the enemy being always inclined to pursue in the original direction. The crew were at their various diving-stations. The silence was almost oppressive ; nothing could be heard except the faint sound of the horizontal rudder, or the movement of the wheel. The boat was travelling, so far as possible, without noise. All the machinery that could be dispensed with was stopped, and the engines were running with the minimum of vibration, for water carries far, and the English have excellent listening apparatus with which they can quickly discover the presence of a U-Boat and determine its course. The Commander is at the periscope above ; now and again he snaps out a brief order to the man at the wheel, or raps on the depth-gauge : " Up . . . up . . . up . . . stop ! Down . . . down . . . stop ! Up . . . stop . . . down . . . stop . . . carry on."

This odd succession of orders is all that can be heard of what is going on when the Commander wants to get a glimpse of the upper world through the periscope. Slowly and cautiously he lets it rise until it just appears above the surface, and allows the briefest glance over the water, but it must not rise any higher, or the enemy will notice it, so that the movement of the waves and the slight variations in the boat's depth have to be constantly borne in mind.

What the Commander saw did not appear to be very pleasant ; sharp ears might have heard some service expressions of remarkable vigour fall from his lips. And it was, indeed, not pleasant, for he saw eight enemy trawlers. Two of them, in token that they had successfully picked up our position by their listening apparatus, had hoisted large red flags, and lay with their bows almost exactly on our course. The others, which were somewhat further away, were dashing up at full speed.

" Lower periscope and dive to 30 metres," says the Commander, in a tone hardly above that of conversation.

Accordingly, the boat tilts gently forward, the depth-gauge needle slowly rises, and the boat sinks to the required depth. The needle creeps up, metre by metre : 19 . . . 20 . . . 21 . . . 22 . . .—a sudden shock, and it stops at 24 metres.

"Stop both engines, switch all power off, including the gyro-transmission ; silence in the boat."

We had, without realising it, touched bottom, being much nearer inshore than we had thought. Far from having 40 or 50 metres beneath our keel, the sea-floor was perilously near. There was only one thing to do, which was to follow the example of the proverbial hare and sham dead. Hence the above orders. This was our only hope of escape from a desperate position. Above us were eight trawlers, each equipped with everything that makes a U-Boat sailor's heart beat faster, such as depth-charges, nets, listening apparatus, etc., and below them was a U-Boat lying on the sea-floor at a depth of 24 metres.

Crash ! The first depth-charge ; then two more in rapid succession. The boat quivered in every plate. Most of the glass fitments were cracked by the shock, and it looked as though the next quarter of an hour would decide our fate. The next explosions sounded rather further off. The officer of the watch, Lieutenant Rosenbaum, stands at the compass, recording the times of the explosions in a note-book. The total is fifteen, the last being much fainter than its predecessors ; it looks as though the trawlers have lost us. Then follows a heavy detonation quite near the boat. The lights go out for a moment, and the barometer of our hopes sinks lower. Five minutes later a voice in the control-room says "Thirty-two," apparently referring to the number of depth-charges already exploded ; and another voice adds significantly, "That divides by eight, anyhow." The meaning of which is that, if each trawler had four depth-charges on board, this must have been the last.

We wait. Minutes pass, and there is, in fact, no further

explosion. Once more we must imitate the hare and make a dash for safety as soon as the coast is clear.

The boat comes to life again. Our problem now, and indeed our only chance, is to manœuvre her towards the surface with the minimum amount of noise—that is, by using compressed air instead of engine power, and so make our escape under water. This operation depends, in the main, on the Chief Engineer and the control-room mate, but there is no U-Boat manœuvre in which the entire crew does not play its part. And so it is in this case. Every man is at his diving-station ready to rush from one end of the boat to the other to redress the balance if she dips too steeply by the bow or stern. There could be no better instance of the close co-operation of a U-Boat crew.

This difficult manœuvre was effected in a masterly manner by carefully blowing the diving-tanks and gradually opening the valves. After a few anxious moments the boat was moving slowly along at a depth of 10 metres, and the Commander cautiously pushed the periscope just above the surface to see what was happening "up above." He swung it round quickly once, and, having made sure there was no imminent peril, he turned it again more slowly and carefully and inspected the field of vision.

"Thank the Lord!" said the Commander; but no one understood except the officer of the watch and the Navigating Officer, who were standing beside him on the conning-tower. But they said nothing, for the moment had come when the Commander at the periscope stands, and must stand, alone, and cannot share his burden. The brave fellows below must wait patiently at their diving-stations while the watcher above observes, ponders, and decides.

The Commander was rightly grateful to the Lord. The eight trawlers were now lying some distance away; they appeared to have been carried off by the current in the meantime, and were now busily searching in the wrong place. They were, therefore, relatively harmless, but from the opposite direction had appeared a group of vessels of various types, which the trawlers had no doubt summoned by wireless, and were preparing to drag the comparatively shallow water with some apparatus that they were towing behind them. They were not far distant, and were approaching the U-Boat on a broad front. It was only possible to evade them if we could succeed in getting round the end of the line nearest to us. Fortunately, the wind had freshened, and the resultant swell allowed of a cautious use of the periscope ; moreover, the enemy would now find it more difficult to locate us by observation from the air or by the help of listening apparatus.

Then followed minutes of fearful tension that seemed eternal, until, at last, a glance through the periscope revealed that we had indeed circumvented the enemy unless they changed course, and the Commander whistled a few bars of " The Rose of Stamboul."

The silence in the boat was paralysing. There was nothing to be done but wait. The crew listened intently. What would they hear next ? The grating sound of the net as it caught the hull, the detonation of depth-charges, or what ? Perhaps nothing. The interior of the boat was brightly lit, and one could not help but think : "What if the enemy could see us now." The whirr of the electric engines driving the propellers was faintly audible. We could not put on any more power, or there would be too much noise, and if we went any slower we should not be able to get away. Such moments of inaction and self-questioning seem eternal.

With an extremity of caution the periscope was raised so that we could catch a glimpse of how we lay. The seconds during which the water in the periscope grows gradually brighter as the tip of it approaches the surface, until it finally emerges, are, in such encounters as this, some of the most nerve-racking that a man can endure. On one occasion the periscope came up so near an enemy vessel that it looked as though there were an enormous storm cloud in the sky, the fact being that the periscope was right alongside the other ship's hull.

The periscope emerged at last, and the Commander swung it rapidly round to see if the coast was fairly clear, and he observed the enemy ships in a group a mile or so away and searching for us there. The Commander heaved a mighty sigh of relief ; once more there was a hope of shaking off this horde of pursuers. Every fresh glance through the periscope made it certain that we were slowly but surely getting away from them, and the aeroplanes that appeared from time to time did not alarm us, for a good deal of wind had got up in the meantime, and the rough sea would prevent any airman sighting the shadow of our boat beneath the surface. It was now past noon, and the chase had lasted eight hours. At a rough estimate, about sixty vessels had been engaged in a vain attempt to catch one German U-Boat.

It must certainly be admitted that the English showed us great respect wherever we appeared, especially in the Irish Sea. Each one of us might well be proud of the fact that there were now two enemy ships per head of the crew. We could not ask for a more honourable reception.

12

THE WHITE SHIP

By

Navigating Officer Grassl

TRADE between England and Norway could not be allowed to stop during the war, for the exchange of commodities between the two countries had become an absolute necessity for the English. As the customary routes were barred by mines and U-Boats, the English used a fresh route to the north. Every day more and more small steamers, mostly of Norwegian and Danish nationality, collected off the Shetlands Isles, and thence proceeded under escort to the north coast of Norway, between Holmengraa and Hellisö. This route was also used by the English to send supplies to their Russian Allies, who in 1917 were in serious difficulties. It was Germany's task to intercept this traffic.

On a glorious day in July, 1917, U 67 put out to sea from Emden Harbour, circled round the island of Borkum, and made for the west coast of Denmark. The shadowy outline of Heligoland soon appeared on the horizon ; seagulls swooped down to greet us and escorted the boat as far as the island of Sylt, which we passed in the late afternoon, where we could see through our binoculars all the lively doings of a seaside resort in summer. But this peace-time picture soon vanished, and darkness descended on the heaving sea.

In the early hours of morning we caught four Danish steamers, from whose cargoes we extracted several parcels containing women's model hats from England.

For the next fortnight we patrolled the coast of Norway—

northwards as far as the North Fjord, southward as far as Hellisö. Day after day we swept the seas, up and down and round about, but not a single enemy ship did we sight. However, we were all able to enjoy the scenery of Norway. The high mountain ridge to the north of the fjord, called Ungedal, which dominates the whole landscape with its colossal rocky wall, is an unforgettable sight and a magnificent background to the fjord. In the hottest summer the glaciers reach from

A northerly course towards the midnight sun.

Hohenkar right down to the sea ; indeed, in July the temperature is almost tropical though the nights are cooler. Sunset in these latitudes is a truly magic spectacle; the sun sinks like a great fiery ball beneath the waves, which then burst into a glittering display of rainbow colours. The lighthouses, too, with their variously intermittent flashes, and the twinkling lights on the high mountain paths, made so lovely a picture in this clear night air that we were lost in silent wonderment.

But the picture is quite different when storms come down from the north-west. Huge waves dash furiously against the cliffs and fall, thundering and roaring, in showers of foam.

At such times the navigation of these fjords is very dangerous, and careful pilots and captains will seldom come near the coast. Fishing, so profitable an industry to the population, is then abandoned, and the trawlers, with their deep-sea trawling nets, lie hidden in harbour.

One afternoon, about three o'clock, while we were on a northward course, a certain white ship stirred our curiosity. She had three masts, of which the foremast only was square-rigged, a curved bow ornamented with carving, and a gilt figure-head. Her rig was that of a three-masted schooner. There was no one at the wheel on the after deck, and no ladders or lifeboats, and her reddish-white paint made us very suspicious. As the vessel was in neutral waters we assumed she was not armed, but we were much struck to notice that she sailed every day from north to south and back again. Day after day we watched her. She never left neutral waters and, as she passed, always signalled greetings which we returned. The white ship became a familiar riddle. There were all sorts of speculations, and even bets, as to the nature and occupation of the vessel. Opinions differed greatly and often led to heated argument. Was she a survey ship, a pleasure yacht, a trawler, a U-Boat decoy? None of us could tell.

At last our Commander decided to clear up the mystery. We came nearer inshore so as to pass within half a knot of neutral water. The Navigating Officer kept a look-out to starboard, and a leading seaman and a seaman to port. We were moving at twelve knots, when one of the port watch suddenly yelled that the white ship had turned and was bearing down on us.

Hardly had he spoken, when we heard the report of two guns.

" Hard a-port ; full speed ahead ; close bulkheads ; man the pumps ! "

Five dreadful seconds ! We clutched the conning-tower casing.

" By God, they've got us ! . . . No, they've missed ! "

" Hard a-starboard. Rudder midships ! "

The Commander wanted to chase the decoy ship and blow her out of the water, but she turned away to port, hoisted the English flag, and made for the neutral waters of the fjord.

We took some time to calm down after this display of duplicity and cowardice. However, we had survived, though we had come very near to death, and we felt we must celebrate this renewal of our lives. The Commander produced a keg of Geneva, a vast ham, and five army loaves, and over this feast, to the accompaniment of a gramophone, we soon recovered our composure.

At seven o'clock the same evening we picked up from near at hand the signal of the U-Boat that was to relieve us. After a hearty exchange of greetings we told them of our adventure and commended the white ship to their particular attention. Then, having wished each other good luck and good-bye, we set off homewards.

13

BETWEEN A SINKING SHIP AND THE BOTTOM OF THE SEA

By

Leading Seaman Karl Stolz

WHEN our newly-commissioned UB 88 had repeatedly carried out the prescribed diving and manœuvring tests, she was ordered to put to sea on June 13th, 1918. To the Commander's disgust, a little company of wives and sweethearts turned up from Kiel and the surrounding district, and the cables were cast off to the accompaniment of many waving handkerchiefs.

UB 88 set out at full speed on a northerly course. Night was falling.

I was at the wheel, and thus able to enjoy the lovely June evening as I kept a look-out for the buoy that marked our route, letting my eyes wander now and then towards the evening horizon and the Schleswig coast. It grew gradually darker; I was already steering by compass, and was glad to note that we were not making for the Kaiser Wilhelm Canal, but northward to the Little Sound. The passage from the Canal to the German Gulf and the North Sea was not very popular in the Imperial Navy: Tommy had snapped up too many of our U-Boats in those waters.

As I was enjoying the stillness of the evening I heard behind me a sudden movement of alarm. The officer of the watch was staring into the distance through his binoculars; suddenly he shouted down the speaking-tube: " Report to Commander lighted waterspout to port ! " This sounded interesting.

Being at the wheel, I had no binoculars and had to search for this singular natural phenomenon with the naked eye. I could see nothing, and Hein, the aft look-out man, refused to let me have a look through his glasses. The Commander threw aside the Navigating Officer's maps and hurried up on deck, but could at first distinguish nothing. In a minute or two, however, the set expression on the officer's face darkened into gloom, as the Commander suddenly smiled genially and remarked :

" That's not a lighted waterspout ; that's the moon ! "

Far away on the horizon a bright streak of light was visible ; it increased with every second, and finally emerged from the waves in the form of a slender crescent. The young officer had received his baptism of fire at the very beginning of the voyage. It was no doubt to dispel the delighted expressions on the faces of the crew that he offered a new dollar to the man who first sighted a ship in the blockade zone.

Our boat was making its way through the relatively narrow passage between Germany, or, rather, what was then still Germany, and Denmark. Some distance away we could see a broad expanse of light on the Danish coast ; it was the large town of Esbjerg blazing into the night. Why not ? She had nothing to fear from air or sea. To the right of us, the coast was shrouded in darkness. We knew, of course, that there, too, life went on, but only under cover of the night. On our boat, too, the lights were turned off or lowered ; for we had entered the war area.

Our thudding engines drove us onwards through the North Sea. It was now daylight, and we were confronted with an unpleasant-looking mine-barrier : some of them were rocking on the surface, plainly visible ; others, we knew, were anchored out of sight. But we made our way safely through them and drew in towards England. Not a single vessel had been sighted as we turned northwards, a few miles off the English coast, when suddenly Lieutenant Schmitz's promised dollar looked like being won.

"Smoke-cloud four points on starboard bow."

This brought the Commander on deck, and no sooner had he got into the conning-tower than we were promptly ordered below :

"Diving-stations ! Flood tanks ! Periscope-depth ! "

All this happened so quickly that it could not be precisely decided to whom the promised dollar should fall. The crew swung themselves down the conning-tower to the control-room and hurried to their posts ; a fusillade of orders followed.

I had to abandon my peaceful consumption of a plate of beans and bacon, and in an instant was at my action-station at the wheel. The main periscope dynamo began its rhythmical hum, as the periscope was dipped and raised to make sure that only the tip of it showed above the surface. The Navigating Officer appeared in the conning-tower with his bearings apparatus, and the boat was at last moving steadily at the required depth of $10\frac{1}{2}$ metres, when the following orders rang out :

"Clear first and third tubes."

"First and third tubes clear."

"Torpedo depth—$4\frac{1}{2}$ metres."

". . . $4\frac{1}{2}$ metres it is."

"Twenty degrees more to port."

All this and much more I had to repeat ; and I had to keep a very accurate course, for the man at the wheel really aims the torpedo-tube, which is a fixed part of the vessel, and the whole operation is dependent on his skill.

"Five men ready to dress the boat ! "

These five men are our movable ballast. The Chief Engineer cannot get his pumps to work as quickly as these smart fellows can dash from the control-station into the bows and thus compensate for the lost weight of the fired torpedo. Otherwise the bow would tip out of the water at a most inopportune moment.

"Ten degrees more to port ; Warrant Officer, note— s.s. *Farewell*, 2,000 tons, two funnels, deep in cargo."

("Good God," thought I; "we must be pretty near if he can read the ship's name.")

"Lower periscope; dive full speed to 20 metres; every man forward." . . . "Hard a-port; both engines full speed ahead."

A destroyer, perhaps? It looked as if we had nearly collided with something. And, indeed, the periscope was not lowered in time; a grinding sound was heard, which meant the end of that too inquisitive periscope.

What had happened was that our victim had made an unexpected turn which we could not follow, and we had had to dive under her. The only thing was to keep quiet and see whether the enemy had noticed us. The rhythmic beat of the steamer's engines and propellers suddenly stopped, so we ventured up again to have another look at our friend through the spare periscope. All this seemed to happen in a flash.

"Clear first tube. . . . Fire!"

. . . Hit!

"Every man forward. . . . Dive to 40 metres . . . to the bottom. . . . Silence in the boat. . . ."

When the depth-gauge recorded 38 metres the boat bumped very audibly on a sandy bottom; we were on the sea-floor and there we lay. Engines, pumps, compass-dynamo—all were turned off so that not a sound should betray the position of the boat. But, although we lay in utter silence, there was plenty of noise in our immediate neighbourhood. Enemy patrol-boats were already dashing about above us and persistently dropping their noisy visiting-cards. Dozens of depth-charges set for 30 metres exploded with every variety of detonation over our heads.

After half an hour or so the patrols decided that they had better give up, and the bombardment ceased. Since the order "Silence in the boat," none of us had left our action-stations; I was still standing at the wheel in the conning-tower, entering up the steering-book, in which all changes, of course—depth, engine speed, with the times at which they were made, and, last but not least, complete details of all torpedo actions —have to be recorded. In such encounters the man at the wheel needs a ready pen.

As I stood writing, I heard a faint ticking sound ; I put the listening microphones to my ears and heard the same sound, much intensified. At first I did not pay much attention ; then an unpleasant suspicion crept into my mind. I mentioned it to the Commander, who was still in the conning-tower, and he shouted down to the engine-room : " Both engines half speed ahead." The boat moved forward jerkily, then stopped. " Both engines half speed astern." More jerks, and a sudden stop. After the silence, the noise of the engines was quite exhilarating. Every moment I expected to hear the crash of a depth-charge, or the scraping of a grapnel across the hull.

" I believe the steamer is on top of us," I said to the Commander.

" Looks like it," he answered, and shouted down to the control-station : " Ask the Chief to come up, please."

When the Chief Engineer appeared, the Commander said in low tone :

" That steamer seems to have sunk on top of us ; don't let the crew know yet. We'll wait a bit and then see if we can get up to the surface by using compressed air as well as the engines. If not, we must try to get out of the boat somehow."

The crew were now told they could leave their diving-stations. With the exception of the men at the compass and in the engine-room, they all went to their bunks, some to make up for lost sleep, others to play cards or read a book from the *Reclam* library.

All was peace, except for me. It was agonising to realise that the masts or keel of a steamer were lying across our hull, and our chances of escape were very small ; and the Commander must have felt no less. I had once caught sight of his family in Kiel, a charming wife and two pretty children, and I could well imagine that he, too, would rather be in

Kiel than at the bottom of the sea. However, the afternoon wore slowly to an end, until it was thought that the patrol-boats had almost certainly given up the search.

It was half-past seven in the evening when we were ordered to diving-stations, and the compressed air was slowly injected into the tanks. In the interval, the tide had turned ; it was now just high tide, and the depth-gauge showed 42 metres. The boat rose very gradually to 40½ metres and then stopped. More compressed air was let in, but she would not move. We were clearly caught in the steamer's rigging. Both engines were run at full speed ahead for a time, until the lamps grew redder and redder. The electric accumulator battery was now running down. Just as we were growing desperate, Neptune himself, perhaps, came to our rescue, and shifted the rope that had caught us ; the boat moved upwards. Our struggles were over, and we rose at half speed to periscope-depth. The coast must have been clear, as the boat was ordered to the surface : the Diesel engines were started, and the look-outs went up on to the conning-tower.

We gasped with relief to find ourselves alive.

" Both engines full speed ahead ; recharge motors."

But the coast was not yet altogether clear. One patrol-boat which was still cruising in the neighbourhood dashed towards us with thick bursts of smoke, and wished us good evening with its 5-inch gun. In our condition, with empty accumulators, we could not be drawn into a fight with her and the destroyer flotilla that she must already have summoned. So we had to try to disappear as quickly as we could in the gathering twilight ; we set a rapid zig-zag course and soon escaped.

Thus, under difficulties, we sank our first steamer. When night fell we made our way northwards, round England and Ireland, and out into the Bay of Biscay, where we set ourselves to sinking American munition ships and transports.

14

DISTURBED NIGHTS IN THE OCEAN DEPTHS

By

Navigating Officer Grassl

It was early April of 1918. UC 70 was lying in Bruges harbour, which was then half empty. The seagulls were screaming in shrill complaint at the scanty refuse from the few ships in port. From time to time we would wave good luck to an outgoing vessel, or a welcome to a returning one ; or listen to the adventures of the new arrivals. But for the most part we were bored, and waited impatiently to be ordered to sea. We had not come to idle about while thousands of our comrades were at grips with the enemy. Every one of us longed to be up and doing.

When one day the order came to load up with mines, we were delighted. How we toiled ! The man next to me, a real old black-haired sea-dog, muttered incantations over each mine as he slung it into the shaft : " I hope you'll send a fat Englishman to the bottom," he said to the last one. Our sister-ship, UC 68, which had shared our long wait, was also getting ready for a voyage.

It was a clear, calm April night when the two boats, escorted by two destroyers, set off down the Bruges Canal. At last we had our wish : we were going to meet the enemy, England. About ten miles off the western estuary of the Scheldt, near the Wandelaar light-ship, the two destroyers wished us good luck and turned back ; and soon after we parted from UC 68.

But before we could get at the enemy we had to dispose of our mines. Our orders were to extend the chain of mines already laid by our predecessors along the Belgian-Dutch coast between Ymuiden and the Maas light-ship, off the Hook of Holland-Rotterdam Canal. This was no light task for those in charge of the boat, especially for the Navigating Officer, since it involved cruising under water by night, and so locating the last mine in the existing chain. Moreover, as the level of the sea is constantly changing owing to the ebb and flow of the tides along the coast, the mines have to be fixed at such a point below the surface that a ship cannot pass over them at high tide without exploding them ; nor must they float on the surface at low tide, in which event they could be destroyed by gun-fire.

From Wandelaar we steered north as far as latitude 52 degrees 20 north, off Ymuiden, to the north-west of Amsterdam. The darkness grew more and more intense. The look-out men tried to pierce the gloom with straining eyes : not a ship to be seen ; not the faintest shadow on the waste of waters.

At eleven o'clock, about 20 miles from land, we dived to what we calculated would be the level of the mine-field, and laid our course to the south-west in continuation of the existing chain, the termination of which we had succeeded in discovering after three-quarters of an hour's search. The crew were all at their posts ; the look-out men were listening intently and the mine-layers were awaiting orders.

It was exactly midnight when the order " Prepare to lay mines " rang out in the Commander's sharp, clear voice.

" Aye, aye, Sir."

The first mine sped from the shaft, plunged gurgling downwards and anchored itself automatically to the bottom. One after the other, at regular intervals, the whole number followed in rapid succession ; and the six shafts had soon deposited their complement of three mines each.

Our first task thus successfully accomplished, we kept under water for another 20 miles to the south-east, and then, breaking surface, laid a course north-north-east towards the English coast, where we hoped to find many victims.

K 2

A cold wind made us shiver, and suddenly we ran into a squall of snow and hail. By three o'clock in the morning we had safely crossed the mine-barrier between Terschelling and Flamborough Head, and reached the mine-free area off the coast. The Commander decided to dive to the bottom to provide the wearied crew with a well-earned rest. The Navigating Officer had misgivings ; he thought it certain that a mine-sweeper or a destroyer would be unpleasantly active in these waters, and that the boat would be exposed to great risk. However, in his opinion, the risk was just as great further out at sea among the mine-fields ; while here we were excellently placed for attacking the convoy of five or six steamers, escorted by a small cruiser and four torpedo-boats, that passed that point every day from the south.

We accordingly dived and lay on the bottom in mine-free water about 3 miles from Flamborough Head. The exhausted crew were soon snoring in various keys ; only the Navigating Officer had to apply himself to his nautical calculations. Deep silence surrounded him as he sat busily at work ; and he had been entering up his records for something like an hour, when he suddenly stopped and listened. A noise—of propellers—from the south. He stood listening as though turned to stone. Nearer and nearer came the sound, and it grew more and more distinct.

" A destroyer, by God ! " said the Navigating Officer, and ran to wake the Commander.

" Well ? "

" There's something wrong, Sir."

" What do you mean ? "

" Listen."

At that moment we could hear grapnels grinding across our hull. But our luck was in ; the depth-charges, which are detonated by electricity, could not have been set. In any case, the danger was over for the moment.

But twenty minutes later the same sound was again audible, this time from a northerly direction. Nearer and nearer came the destroyer, and suddenly dashed over us with a roar of its propellers. Our boat quivered and shot up to the surface ; then it plunged downwards and crashed on to the sea-floor. Plates and cups and everything movable leapt from tables and shelves, and the crew rolled in confusion on the floor. When calm had been restored and everyone had counted and felt his bones, we all looked at each other. We were shaken but unhurt. Then a new fear flashed through our minds. Supposing our boat had been so damaged that it could not move ? Were we, in effect, buried alive ? Monstrous thought.

The hull of the boat was minutely examined ; not a sign of damage could be found. Each engine was exhaustively tested. We breathed again when the Commander told us that the main and reserve periscopes had been badly damaged and bent, but that the boat was quite uninjured. But every one of us had now to do his utmost to get us out of this awkward situation. We could not possibly come to the surface at this point, and as the periscopes could no longer be hoisted, we were sightless. We proceeded under water for 30 knots, until at last we ventured to emerge. Anxiously we searched the surrounding sea and the horizon : not a ship in sight.

We now turned southwards at full speed, and soon reached the Terschelling banks ; we were travelling along the Dutch coast as the shades of twilight began to creep up. The moon shone fitfully down on us through shifting wreaths of mist, and also made us an easier mark for the enemy. A torpedo-boat flotilla, hardly discernible in the mist, fortunately did not observe us. Soon afterwards, a thudding roar above our heads announced an enemy airman, who was shortly joined by a second and a third. We had to run for it, and only escaped unscathed under cover of the mist which blew up between us and our pursuers. About 10 miles off the entrance to the Bruges Canal German patrol-boats came into view, and the brightly-lit Wandelaar light-ship helped us to find our way home.

When we got into dock the crew were given twelve hours' leave, and two new periscopes were fitted.

*   *   *   *   *

At ten o'clock in the evening a whistle blew from the deck of UC 70. It had been good to feel the solid earth beneath our feet again, but now the time was up ; and not a man of the crew was missing. The seamen were on deck, and the mechanics at their engines and dynamos. All the lights on deck were extinguished ; only an occasional flash of a torch betrayed where the cables were being cast off.

Noiselessly the boat glided down the Bruges Canal to Zeebrugge, and at 4 a.m. we passed the outer gates. We laid a course north-north-west through neutral waters to a point 30 miles west of Terschelling light-ship. Thence for some distance we were passing through fishing-grounds, and had to take great care not to foul any nets ; finally, still keeping on a north-westerly course, we reached the latitude of Flamborough Head.

Towards midday, about 30 miles from the English coast, we came up with a small sailing-vessel manned by a crew of four. We approached to within 100 yards of her, asked who she was, what cargo she was carrying, and whether she was armed. The captain assured us that their only cargo was petroleum and fish, and that the boat was not armed. The Commander, thinking that this shabby little cutter could hardly exercise a decisive influence on the issue of the war, was proposing to let her go, when it occurred to me that she might be able to do us a very useful service.

" Have you got a navigating chart ? " I shouted.

" Yes, but we need it ourselves."

When we made them understand that we would give them something in exchange they seemed more affable, and shouted that if we would let them have some biscuits we could come aboard and search their boat and make a copy of the chart at the same time.

We sent three men across in the dinghy with biscuits and a bottle of schnapps ; the chart was brought over to the U-Boat and carefully copied, while the cutter stood by patiently for above an hour. Then an English seaplane appeared ; we flung back their map to them at the end of a rope, and their thanks were borne back to us on the wind. We were delighted to possess a detailed map of the English coast from Flamborough

Our boat was got out and sent across with three men.

Head to Sunderland. Every free channel, every mine-field, and all the submarine nets were exactly indicated.

Towards evening a convoy of four steamers appeared from the north accompanied by two destroyers. We gave chase and chose as our victim the largest of the four, a vessel of about 3,600 tons. She was an easy target, and both the patrol-boats were at the head of the line. She sank at once, and we could distinctly hear the water pouring into the boiler-room. The destroyers dropped a large number of depth-charges, which we could see pretty clearly, being in comparatively shallow water.

The light had nearly gone when we came up to the surface ; dark shadows flickered on the water, and the night wind rustled over the waves ; silently we watched the tumbled water hissing in our wake as we sped northward, keeping pretty close inshore. By daylight we were cruising off the port of Hartlepool. The coast seemed lifeless ; not a glimmer of light nor the faintest fleck of smoke. Still, we could wait ; and we did not wait in vain. About eight o'clock one of the look-out men pointed to southward and shouted :

" Convoy in sight."

I peered over the conning-tower parapet and said : " Where ? "

" There. . . . Can't you see . . . one . . . two . . . three. . . ."

Masts, funnels, bridges, gradually emerged above the horizon, and four steamers with five armed escorts appeared in the lenses of our binoculars.

We dived and stopped about 600 metres from the line of the convoy's approach, and waited for it to reach us, which it did in about half an hour. The best range is from 180 to 200 metres, so we drew a little nearer to the convoy's course. The largest ship was our destined victim, and we dived under the torpedo-boats which were between us and the steamers. In a few minutes we had fired our torpedo at a range of 140 metres. We then dived to 50 metres under the torpedoed steamer, turned to starboard, still keeping under water, and went ahead at full speed for 60 miles. The five torpedo-boats attacked us with such vigour that we had to dive to 70 metres to get out of range of the depth-charges. One boat pursued us for four hours until she realised that the chase was hopeless.

We did not sight another vessel during the whole of that day. In a clear night of stars we laid a northerly course towards Sunderland ; the long night watches wore gradually on, and with the daylight we hoped we should come upon another victim. At eight o'clock not a smoke-cloud was in sight. " They daren't come out," muttered the Commander, in disgust. At last, two hours later, a convoy hove in sight—four steamers and two destroyers—and put fresh life into us all.

In a few minutes we had sunk a large cargo-steamer of about 6,000 tons ; she must have been partly laden with explosive, as the detonation of the torpedo was unusually loud. The escorts busied themselves with rescuing the crews, and did not pursue us until later, but they soon had to give up the chase. We dived, came up again about midday, turned westward, and cruised about until daybreak.

The next morning saw us again off Sunderland. A large fast steamer with three huge funnels and two masts, a 25,000 tonner at least, was steaming broadside on across the roadstead. The Commander licked his lips at such a target. " We had better torpedo her at once," he said, thinking aloud. But the Navigating Officer and the Officer of the Watch were of opinion that this would be risky as we were so near the shore guns ; moreover, there was not sufficient depth—13 metres— in which to dive. If we torpedoed her, she would merely settle on the sea-bottom ; she could be easily raised in such shallow water and towed into dock. But we should never leave that roadstead alive. Added to which, the distance and the misty morning air made it at least possible that what we saw was an optical illusion. All things considered, the Commander decided not to attack. Unseen, as we had come, we turned away eastwards. We had to spend a whole day and night on the surface to charge our accumulators and prepare some fresh torpedoes.

A clear and sunny morning ; we were lying 10 miles out of the Humber estuary, watching the entrance to Kingstown. Far away in the distance we sighted a sailing-vessel, apparently Danish or Norwegian, making for Kingstown, and we chased and stopped her. She refused to give her nationality.

" Where are you from ? "

" Newport News, with coal."

We told the captain, who spoke Danish and Norwegian alternately, to send a boat across ; but he said his boat leaked and refused.

" He'd better look out," said a man standing beside me ; " the Commander won't stand much more of this."

We lowered our boat and sent three men across. The ship was thoroughly searched, and to our amazement we discovered that she was carrying a mixed cargo of explosive, sulphur, and petroleum. We backed for 200 metres, and the Commander shouted through the megaphone :

" Lower your boat and get away from the ship at once ; we shall open fire in two minutes." The crew—there were only four of them—tumbled into the lifeboat ; one, an oldish man, no doubt the owner of the ship, wept at leaving her. In his distracted state he steered the dinghy right across the line of fire ; we waved him back and signed to him to get behind us. Owing to the dangerous nature of the cargo, we backed another 100 metres before firing a torpedo.

" First and second tubes ready. . . . Fire ! "

A huge sheet of flame shot up and enveloped the ship ; we heard the masts crack and fall. The petroleum burned for a long while on the surface of the water. It was fine weather, and the crew were well able to save themselves. However, we were not to escape pursuit ; a destroyer soon dashed up at full speed. We dived, and resumed our course northwards along the coast.

About two o'clock, as we were proceeding at a depth of 29 metres, we could hear a steamer coming up behind us, making, like ourselves, for the mine-free channel. We swung round 500 metres off our course, rose, manœuvred into position, and fired our torpedo at 200 metres. The shot was a good one, and the ship sank in less than twenty minutes. The crew got away in safety.

Once again we lay off Flamborough Head, and a convoy was not long in coming. Our purpose was to fire a bow torpedo at

200 metres ; but a bow shot was impossible as we had got too near the target. So the Commander ordered a stern shot. Scarcely had the torpedo left the tube than it plunged into the mud and did not explode. We went fast aground. It was indeed fortunate that our shot did not come off, for it took us half an hour to get the boat afloat again.

" Herr Grassl," said the Commander, standing at the periscope, feeling cheerful now that the boat was safely on its way again, " just look through the periscope a minute. . . . Do you see the English bathing beauties ? "

" Yes. . . . I daresay they don't know there's a war on," said that elderly seaman who had sailed all the oceans of the world. There was a quizzical humour in his deep voice that helped him over many hard places.

Northward once again. The sun was westering to the horizon. Was the day to end before we had found a victim ? No ! A faint smoke-cloud just then became visible in the distance : a solitary steamer, towed by two smaller ones, was coming straight towards us. We remained on the surface and fired the port torpedo at her ; but she defended herself vigorously, and shells were soon dropping all round us. However, we were too many for her. Three shots and three hits at the waterline finished her ; the other two made off, and we had to chase them for two hours before we sent them, too, to the bottom.

We kept under water for some time, on an easterly course, and then rose, in the belief that our exploits had not yet attracted attention. In this we were wrong ; a destroyer was soon on the spot. Once more we dived and stayed under water for another 55 miles, but the thud of the destroyer's propellers grew louder ; we could not imagine how she managed to keep on our track. She had located us at 8 p.m., and every three or four minutes she dropped one of her devilish eggs, timed to explode at 30 metres.

One of the crew was a cheery weather-beaten old sailor whose jokes always made us forget our perils. On this occasion he posted himself in the conning-tower, produced a note-book and a pencil, and observed :

" Smart lads up there, aren't they ? How many have they dropped till now ? "

" Fifteen," said the other.

He proceeded to make fifteen strokes in his note-book, and a fresh one as soon as another depth-charge was dropped. The destroyer hung on to us, steadily dropping her missiles, and our friend kept a patient record of every one.

" Ninety-six . . . ninety-seven . . ." he counted with a nonchalant air, adding the strokes with his now blunted pencil.

" I expect they want to finish the hundred," said the Navigating Officer.

" Perhaps they're celebrating the birth of an English Crown Prince," said a young sailor with a laugh.

" Ninety-eight . . . ninety-nine . . ."

He waited for the next and possibly the last, but none came. The whole crew burst into a roar of laughter.

" Well, there's no Crown Prince, and it's midnight. Closing time ; I'm off to bed," observed the old sailor dryly.

The destroyer had been chasing us for four hours. It was true that one of our oil-bunkers was leaking, and the traces of oil in our wake no doubt betrayed our course.

Twenty minutes later we rose to the surface ; our pursuer had vanished. We steered east for 40 miles so as to be able to spend the night undisturbed.

Dawn broke ; once more we laid a course for Flamborough Head, and, remaining under water, drew quite near inshore. Our last torpedo lay in the port tube. Suddenly, just as we were rounding the headland, we were brought up by a wreck lying at a depth of 31 metres. The boat stopped with a frightful jolt that flung us all to the floor.

The engines were at once switched off ; the boat was slowly sinking by the stern. We then set the engines at full speed and made frantic efforts to jerk ourselves free. We tried to clear the after diving-tank and fill the forward tank, and the crew rushed aft to help to trim the boat. Then we tried to pump out the aft torpedo-tube, and empty the aft ammunition-room and deposit its contents forward. All this took time, and it was all quite useless. We should have given up hope without our cheery old friend's encouragement. Hour after hour we laboured in vain ; the air grew steadily worse, and the crew began to despair. For the last time we purified the air as well as we could ; we had plenty of oxygen, but no fresh air. The men grew more and more impatient ; no one thought of food ; and even schnapps, that trusty comforter, was forgotten. We saw our end draw near.

As a final chance, the Commander asked for a volunteer to get outside the boat and examine its position. It was, in fact, possible, by using the conning-tower as a valve, for a man to get out of the boat, and with the help of a diving-lamp he might have some chance of finding out what was wrong. A young sailor at once volunteered.

But before resorting to extremity we put our utmost efforts into one last manœuvre. We set both propellers at full speed, and then swung the stern over with a sharp tilt to the right ; then back again to port, and so backwards and forwards four times, while the crew dashed from side to side of the boat. In this way we should either free the bow or break it off. The first manœuvre failed, but when we had managed to trim the boat to a fairly even keel by the help of the after tank, emptied the fresh-water tank to lighten the boat still further, and got the engines to full speed, while the crew leapt wildly from side to side, there was a sudden snapping sound as though a rope had given way. The boat jerked backwards and lay level on the sea-floor. Saved !

The Commander had the boat carefully tested for possible leaks or any other damage that could be ascertained from within. As soon as it was clear that she was uninjured and could rise and dive as usual, we thought we might venture to attack a convoy that was approaching from the south. Before we did so, the boat was thoroughly ventilated through the conning-tower hatch.

Although it took us two hours to reach our attacking-point, we had no opportunity in the interval of coming to the surface and inspecting the outside of our hull ; and the look-outs and each successive man at the wheel reported that UC 70 did not obey her helm so well as usual. It was difficult to get her round to starboard, and she had a tendency to swing round again to port. It was suggested to the Commander that we had better not make another attack, as the uncertain steering made it doubtful whether we could take proper aim ; but he would not listen.

With heavy hearts we attacked the almost unguarded convoy. The port tube was fired. . . . A miss !

And now for home !

At four o'clock the next morning we came to the surface. To our consternation we observed that about 2 metres of the boat's bow, from deck to keel, was bent to starboard at an angle of 45 degrees. It was very fortunate that our last torpedo had been in our port tube ; if it had been in the starboard one, we should have sunk our own boat.

We had to go all the way to Bruges on the surface. Luckily, we got home safely, proud of our perilous but successful voyage. For our sister boat, UC 68, we waited in vain ; she never returned from her attempt to break through into the Channel. UC 70 was also sunk in the Channel a year and a quarter later, destroyed on August 28th, 1918, by depth-charges from an English torpedo-boat.

15

BURIED ALIVE

By

Leading Seaman W. Schlichting

The telephone rang insistently in the U-Boat headquarters at Kiel. The Naval News Station at Friedrichsort was on the line, and reported that a number of U-Boats and their supply-ship *Meteor* had been observed entering harbour. Shortly after came a call from U-Boat Records, inquiring whether a certain boat, of which a description was given, had returned with the rest. She was not on the list. The stations at Friedrichsort and Bülk had been rung up, but nothing was known there. The U-Boat Training School, to which the boat in question was attached, stated that she had gone out on a practice trip to the Apenrade Fjord, but should long since have returned. In the absence of any further information it seemed only too likely that she had met with an accident.

How was it possible to search for so small an object in so vast an area? By aeroplane. My first act was to call up the aeroplane station at Hottenau; and in less than a quarter of an hour four machines were engaged in an active search. The weather was luckily fine. In a short time a report came in from Hottenau that an aeroplane had sighted the missing boat; it was lying on the sea-floor in the centre of the Channel near the exit. As the sun was shining brightly, the water was very transparent, and the dark hull could be clearly seen against the whitish ooze.

Then I did some frantic telephoning. I began by trying to get hold of S.M.S. *Vulkan*, the submarine salvage ship; it seemed ages before the *Vulkan* replied, and yet it was only a matter of minutes. She reported that she was proceeding at full speed to the scene of the accident, and the *Meteor* had also been ordered to stand by.

Both ships set feverishly to work. The divers laboured manfully in the sticky ooze to get the hawsers round the U-Boat's hull, but the mud was so thick that it was hours before they could get the cables into position. We succeeded in communicating by knocks with seven of the imprisoned crew, and learned that all the others were dead. The supply of air was almost exhausted, and unfortunately the potash cartridges were in another compartment ; the bulkhead door was holding, and there was no fear at present that the water would get in. Slowly, in a series of jerks, the crane raised the shattered boat ; the periscope was already above the surface, when, with a rending crack, the two forward hawsers split like tinderwood.

All our labours had been in vain. Undismayed, the divers began their work once more. The impetus of the falling boat had driven it so firmly into the slime that it was now three-quarters submerged. A whole day passed before the hawsers could again be got under the hull. Our hopes revived as the cables were slowly drawn up, but once more we were to fail. This time all the ropes broke, though they were the strongest available. The knocking signals grew perceptibly weaker. The prisoners had been so full of hope, only to have it snatched from them like this : it was too ghastly to think of. The salvage work had now lasted seventy hours. The weather had been good hitherto, but the sea now grew rough. The *Meteor* had to weigh anchor, and the *Vulkan* was so battered by the waves that it was feared she might spring a leak. But she and her brave divers laboured on alone. She pitched and rolled heavily, and began to drag her anchor. The storm was too great. It was only with the greatest efforts and care that the divers, who were quite worn out, were hoisted on to the deck. The *Vulkan* proceeded slowly homewards, and very nearly added to our disasters by running ashore on the way.

For weeks it was impossible to attempt any salvage operations. The survivors in the boat were undoubtedly all dead. Not until four months later was it possible to raise the boat. She was almost entirely covered with ooze, only the conning-tower being visible. The labour of getting the cables round that wreck was the heaviest that those indefatigable divers had ever undertaken. Slowly the windlasses began to turn, and in a succession of jerks the boat, now enveloped in a garment of green seaweed, emerged to the surface. The cause of the accident was soon discovered. The boat had fouled one of the mines from the mine-barrier off the Apenrade Fjord, which had exploded and sent her to the bottom.

When we returned, we were faced with the dreadful task of opening the boat. The conning-tower hatch was forced ; a burst of choking poisonous air poured out, and the sight of the corpses was terrible. What must the poor fellows have endured before death brought them merciful relief ! What scenes of horror and madness had been enacted in that narrow cabin ! The scratches on the steel walls, the corpses' torn finger-nails, the blood-stains on their clothes and on the walls, bore all too dreadful witness. Carefully, as though they were still alive, they were lifted, put into hammocks, and carried ashore.

The funeral was very impressive. In plain but touching words the chaplain described the life of a U-Boat sailor, who may be called on at any minute to stand before his Creator. We turned away, deeply moved.

The boat was repaired in the dockyard, and did long and useful service ; she sent many thousand tons of shipping to the bottom of the sea.

16

THE SINKING OF THE *ARMENIA*

By
Engine-room Artificer Nikolaus Jaud

As darkness fell, we left Emden and made our way towards Borkum, off which we anchored. Our Commander was sent for by the Flotilla-Captain and given his orders. Before setting out again, a further diving-test was carried out to ensure that the vessel was absolutely watertight and to adjust the trim so exactly that when she lay at rest she swung to and fro with the delicacy of a balance. Then we dived out to sea.

For the first few days we kept a northerly course without encountering a single enemy ship. The sea was calm, and the watch kept a sharp look-out. Suddenly Boatswain Preuss reported a periscope in sight, and the next moment the track of a torpedo, and then another. The boat was swung round with skilful promptitude, and disaster was avoided. The Commander congratulated the men on their watchfulness, and when Boatswain Preuss passed through the oil-room aft we hastened to decorate him with a tin *Pour le Mérite* cross.

When we were safely past the strongly guarded channel between the Shetlands and the Orkneys we laid a course for the west coast of England, where we expected to find an excellent field of operations. Our first victim was a sailing-ship, on its way from Canada to England ; then, at the south-western-most corner of the English coast, we sighted another sailing-ship, a three-master with a cargo of wheat from America. We made her heave-to ; her crew, consisting of a Russian captain and twelve men of no less than seven different nationalities, were allowed to take to the lifeboats.   The vessel was then blown up.

A large fat pig was wandering about the sailing-ship's deck ; we shot it and hauled it into the dinghy.   Our comrades in the U-Boat gave us an uproarious welcome, and the pig was delivered into the tender care of the cook.   He appeared on deck armed with soap, brush and razor, and in a trice, though we could hardly trust our eyes, the pig was soaped and shaved. " Pork and peas," announced the cook on the following day. That was something like a feast ; such a dinner as that made us forget the war for a little while.   But not for long, for the silver-grey hull of a four-funnelled ship was soon sighted.   We made for the great vessel at full speed, and a wild chase began.

A shot crashed out ; the enemy turned to flight, and dashed away into the distance at such a speed that it soon became clear that we were being left behind.   The Commander ordered the engines to be driven as hard as they would go, and yard by yard we began to creep up.   We prayed that the engines might hold out ; if anything went wrong, she would slip through our fingers.   The oil-room hands hung anxiously over both Diesel engines, and one of the men positively stroked the machinery as though to say : " That's right ; keep it up."   The enemy's wireless was working feverishly, and we frantically tried to block it.   It was a fight for life and death.   Very gradually we began to overtake the fugitive.   We opened fire ; but the shots fell short.   More and more power was forced out of the engines ; the engineer kept his eyes fixed on the pressure-gauge and the amperometer, and did rapid calculations, with anguished eyes.   We were now in the fourth hour of the chase.

Nearer and nearer we crept up to the steamer, which was slowly slackening speed, and our shells began to hit.   Smoke was rising from her hull ; the lifeboats hung dangerously tilted across the bulwarks ; the ship was on fire.

" Quick fire," cried the Commander, as the steamer still refused to surrender.   People could be seen jumping overboard, and at last she hoisted a great white flag and stopped.

L 2

A single lifeboat was lowered into the water ; the majority of the crew, niggers for the most part, jumped overboard. The sea around us swarmed with struggling figures. The huge steamer, the Cunarder *Armenia*, lay before us like a wounded animal, shot but not killed. More and more niggers clambered through the portholes and jumped into the water to escape being burnt to death. We sent out an S.O.S. to any English ships in the neighbourhood : " S.S. *Armenia* sunk ; pick up survivors at once."

With the moans and shrieks of the niggers were mingled the wailing cries of animals—mules intended for the Western Front. They went down with the ship, to which a torpedo dealt the death-blow.

It was the U-Boat, and not the *Armenia*, that set a course for Liverpool. The barometer was falling quickly, and the weather was now overcast. A stiff south-wester swept across the water and stirred up a short, choppy sea that began to break over the deck and the conning-tower. The look-out men were already wearing their storm clothes. The weather grew thicker and the waves roared and crashed against the boat.

" Well, Karl, my lad," said the look-out man to his relief, " a warm bed's better than any amount of fresh air."

" Diving-stations ! "

I took up my post in the control-room, when I heard a sudden cry from the conning-tower. The Boatswain's Mate crashed down from the conning-tower to the control-room, followed by the Navigating Officer ; the Commander slammed the hatch, and the Boatswain's Mate sank to the floor unconscious.

The storm had suddenly reached hurricane force ; the boat pitched forward heavily, and a huge sea swept against the conning-tower. The Navigating Officer shouted to the Boatswain : " Hold on ! " But the strength of the storm was more than the strength of man. The Navigating Officer broke an arm, and the Boatswain's Mate, who caught his right foot in the companion ladder, dislocated his hip. Fortunately

They went down with the steamer, to which a torpedo dealt the death-blow.

the Commander was just opening the hatch, and was able to drag the unlucky man below. The Boatswain's Mate was given a strong injection of morphia, and the Second Officer set the Warrant Officer's arm in splints made from cigar boxes. The Second Officer claimed to know something of surgery, but the arm had to be broken again later.

We made haste homewards with our injured men; but it was not until a fortnight later that the sight of Heligoland harbour promised them rest and proper treatment.

17

A PARTICULARLY UNPLEASANT EXPERIENCE

By

Leading Seaman Karl Stolz

On a clear evening in January, UC 14, rocking gently on a mild North Sea swell, swung her slender bow round the long mole that guards the sluice-gates of Zeebrugge against the often angry waters outside. The red and green position lights were extinguished, for beyond the mole the boat was in the war-zone, and Tommy's lively little chasers were waiting for her in the shallow water off the coast.

It was soon warm in the engine-room, for when both the oil and electric engines were running at full speed no one could complain of cold, though the purity of the air stood, of course, in inverse relation to its warmth. When I was comfortably settled below for a quiet chat with my friend Willi, a stoker on the third watch, I was more than disgusted to hear the shouted order : " Machine-gun on deck ; man the gun ! "

I hurried up the ladder so as to get my little sprinkler through the narrow conning-tower before the gun-crew appeared ; the ammunition was handed up to me and the machine was soon set up. A few handfuls of cartridges and I was ready for an interview with Tommy. The small 8·8 was quickly cleared for action, and we were now ready to slip through the shallow water at top speed.

" I suppose you know," said the Commander, " that there are a crowd of motor-boats hereabouts waiting to put a torpedo into us ? If you see the slightest sign of anything, don't wait for an order—shoot. The main thing is to make a noise ; you can't reckon to hit anything on a night like this."

It had indeed grown very dark. Luckily the moon had not yet risen, and the stars shone with a faint cold glimmer that was reflected in the rocking waves around us. We sped through the shallows, on a north-north-easterly course, at 9 knots. The officer of the watch and a rating kept a look-out ahead to port and starboard, and another rating astern ; I, and the gun's-crew, to right and left. Thus we stood and strained our eyes into the enveloping darkness. It was cold up on the conning-tower, and hour followed hour very slowly on that bitter January night ; we had to keep our brains alert so as not to see things that were not there. Again and again one or other of us was convinced that he saw a submarine-chaser dashing towards us. Little was said, and that only in a whisper. We talked of friends who had gone out on just such a black night as this and had been sunk in the shallows before ever they reached the open sea. We knew that our dear cousins yonder were doing all they could to destroy the U-Boats from Zeebrugge and Ostend before they could get to closer quarters.

But neither the machine-gun nor the 8·8 had spoken by the time we reached open water and the projected scene of operations ; it was now about midnight. This trip was our first under a new Commander ; our old one had gone to Germany to take command of a new and much larger U-Boat. We had been a happy family under " the Old Man," with whom we had made many trips into the Channel and the North Sea ; one for all, and all for one, we had striven hard to serve our Fatherland and our comrades in the front-line trenches, and we naturally looked back with regret on our old Commander. He had never troubled us with senseless drill ; he knew us and we knew him, and we had set our minds to sinking all the ships we could.

What the new Commander might be like we did not know, as he had only turned up in the U-Boats lairs at Bruges a few days before, after a course at the Training School at Kiel.

By half-past eleven we were able to slacken speed, and the orders " Clear gun for diving ; machine-gun and gun-crew below ! " sent us scrambling down the conning-tower. We were glad to escape the now icy cold, and to get below before the alarm-bell rang and made us run for it. I lay down for half an hour in a vacant hammock, and its gentle swaying motion was lulling me into a pleasant doze, when I was roused by a most seamanlike dig in the port ribs.

" Look lively ; five minutes to twelve ! "

Alas, there was no help for it ; I had to get up and take my spell at the wheel.

My old friend Fidje told me to set a course 290 degrees at half-past twelve and handed over the wheel. Fidje was none too wide awake at times ; he stumbled along to the fo'castle so as to get there before the engine-room hands and not have to spend four hours in a damp hammock. The boat was a small one, and as on every voyage we took two or three men with us for training, the space on board was more cramped than even the designer had intended ; indeed, three men had to occupy a mattress about 4 feet wide and 6 feet long, and anyone too late to snatch a place had to sleep across the others' feet.

Fidje had handed over the wheel in a position that, for him, was pretty creditable ; it was only 10 degrees out. By the time the compass was checked, which was done at every change of watch, I had corrected the course, so that Fidje's reputation did not suffer.

Onwards we sped through that January night. Below, all was quiet—at any rate, for U-Boat ears : above, in the conning-tower, three men were on the look-out ; aft, in the engine-room, a mechanic and a stoker were busy winning each other's pay at cards—the two Diesel engines were running at full speed and did not need active attention ; in the control-room a mechanic was manipulating some valves ; and I sat in the centre of the boat at the compass, keeping her steady on her course. If the two forward look-out men had not

smoked so many navy-cuts—or at any rate, had not thought it
funny to puff their disgusting smoke down the speaking-tube,
whence it emerged just at the level of my nose—all would have
been idyllic.

At half-past twelve I slowly altered course to 290 degrees.
The boat kept very steady ; I soon grew bored and began to
doze.   All I could see were the black strokes on the compass
dial, and when the gyro-transmission seemed to stick for a
moment or two, I gave the wheel a little jerk.   Well, well, I
had been on my legs since six o'clock in the morning, and four
hours more seemed a very long while.

The Commander had gone up into the conning-tower
without my noticing him, for I suddenly heard his voice down
the speaking-tube :

" Diving-stations ! "

" Diving-stations ! " I yelled to the sleepers.

" Diving-stations ! " they answered, still bewildered with
sleep, as they dashed to their posts.

" Practice only," came the Commander's voice again.

" Practice only," I shouted in my turn, thinking to myself
that the Old Man would have said that at the start, as a
brief memory of the lost father of the U-Boat family flashed
through my mind.

"All ready, Sir," reported the Chief Engineer to the Commander in the conning-tower.

" Everyone below ! "

The three look-out men came tumbling down to the control-
room.

" Close ventilators ; dive to 40 metres ! "

The boat tilted slowly forward as she answered to the horizontal rudder ; and the indicator of the depth-gauge beside
me began to quiver.

"Report every 5 metres," came the Commander's voice
again.

The depth-gauge needle rose from 4 to 5, and then to 6 ; the
boat slid slowly and gently down by the bow.   The Commander

was the last to come below ; he had plainly got the Training School trick of not closing the conning-tower hatch until just before the boat disappeared. He slammed it down, and a moment after a flood of water began to pour down the hatch. He shouted for the compressed air to be turned on. Here was the water still pouring in, swirling round my feet, and streaming into the bows as the boat dipped forward.

The Commander.

" Ten metres," shouted the man at the horizontal rudder . . . 15 metres. . . ."

" As you were ! Horizontal rudder right over ! Full speed upwards."

But the Engineer was helpless ; the boat was sinking like a stone.

" What's happened to the compressed air ? "

" We've got a pressure of four atmospheres, Sir."

" What the hell's the good of that ? "

" . . . 25 metres ! "

I looked into the fore part of the boat ; there stood my friend Willi at his post by the mine-laying shaft, which had long since been closed. The water had already spread into the engine-room, and was now up to my knees. I kept the boat steady on its course. I was oddly interested in what was going on, and found myself reflecting on the details of my death by drowning.

All this went much more quickly, of course, than I can describe it here. Then I saw Willi turn ; I followed his eyes, and noticed the compressed-air indicator on the port side of the boat recorded 160 degrees. Willi, who was now up to his neck in cold water, grabbed at the valve, and the air shot with a roar into the diving-tanks.

Three seconds later we should all have been drowned or suffocated.

If Willi had wrung his hands, or thought of his sweetheart far away, he would never have noticed that compressed-air valve. We had sunk to 28 metres with the conning-tower open, but the boat now leapt to the surface like a balloon. Never could human beings have been more thankful than our soaked and bedraggled little company. The boat was soon pumped clear of water. But suddenly the whole interior was filled with a greenish choking vapour—chlorine gas from the water that had flooded the electric battery.

We were all ordered on deck except the man at the wheel and an engine-room mechanic. We shuddered at the thought of facing the bitter air in our soaked garments ; but a minute later, as I and the chief engine-room mechanic stumbled coughing and choking on to the deck, the pure air seemed heavenly.

And so homewards. We made our way through the shallows undisturbed and landed the boat safely in dock.

What had happened ? Why, the Commander, with the intention of making sure that the clamps on the conning-tower hatchway were in the open position, had, in the darkness, turned the wheel that operated them in the wrong direction ;

they were therefore in the closed position, and when the hatch was lowered it would not catch. However, the Commander took no harm from his ducking ; and later on we helped him to sink many a troopship and many a hospital-munition-transport.

18

A U-BOAT DECOY

By

Wireless Operator Haidt

" Stand by ! Cast off ! Both engines full speed ahead ! "

Orders rang out in quick succession, and in a few minutes U 54 had slipped through the sluice-gates. It was a glorious Sunday in spring—April 21st, 1918. Our new Commander, an experienced and successful officer, who had been First Officer of the Watch on U 57 and had then commanded UB 34, was taking us on a trial voyage to Heligoland.

Four days later, on the following Thursday, we passed through the Kiel Canal into the Baltic, and at one o'clock were lying by the quay-side at Sonderburg. The first stage of our voyage had begun.

" Five and a half hours' shore-leave " ; this was news that aroused general enthusiasm. At the Old Man's wish we went ashore in our deep-sea outfit, and what must to a soldier have seemed a very motley company was soon roving the streets of Sonderburg : officers and men all arrayed in fur caps, jerseys, sea-boots, sou'westers, and leather coats—an attire scarcely suited to telephone-heroes in a garrison town, indispensable as it might be for service on a submarine. We were all in the highest spirits and ready to go through fire and water for the Old Man.

It so happened that we fell in with a captain of infantry, who had very likely never seen the front, and smartly saluted. He stopped, glared at us, and said :

" Do you mean to say you're soldiers ? "

" Yes, Sir ; U-Boat men under orders for the next world,"
replied our tall leading seaman, Knud Iversen, from Apenrade,
and clicked his heels. He could do it better than the rest of
us, as in peace-time he was a Schleswig-Holstein *Musketier.*
The land-rat went on his way, shaking his head and muttering
something about " Pirates."

We were to sail at a quarter to seven that evening, but there

We made our way through the Kaiser-Wilhelm Canal.

was a pleasant episode before we did so. It had got about in
the little town that a U-Boat was lying in harbour, which was
quite a novelty for the inhabitants. An eager and excited
crowd assembled on the quay, and the children, of course,
made their way to the front. We collected our last coppers —
for a sailor's purse holds no more when he is off for a long voyage
—and flung them for love of the Fatherland among the little
throng. What scrambling and screams of joy ! A delightful
farewell.

Then we cast off and steered for the Kattegat and the

Skagerrak. On the 28th we were off the southernmost point of
Norway and laid our course for the Orkneys ; on the 30th,
at three o'clock in the morning, we passed Fair Isle between the
Orkneys and the Shetlands.   At seven o'clock a steamer of
2,500 or 3,000 tons, painted black and grey, came into sight.
We attacked under water, fired a torpedo, and a few seconds
later there was a loud explosion. The steamer heeled over ;
the crew got into the lifeboats and rowed away.   Slowly
we approached at periscope-depth. Why didn't she sink ? It
looked suspicious. The ship gradually righted as we came
nearer, and stopped about 80 metres away ; there was not a
sign of life aboard. She carried a single gun astern. We rose
to the surface.

Suddenly the ship came to life. Hidden portholes sprang
open, her deck swarmed with men, the stern gun was manned,
other guns were unmasked and poured a devastating fire on
us, and between the detonations of the shells we could hear
the rattle of machine-guns. A U-Boat decoy !

The steamer had started her engines again, but she was too
near to us for her shells to do us any harm, and the volleys of
machine-gun bullets made no impression upon our armour-
plating. Suddenly the Commander noticed a masked torpedo-
tube aimed at us, from which at that very instant a torpedo
splashed into the water.

" 'Ware torpedo ! " he shouted. " Both engines full speed
ahead ; hard a-port ; compressed air into all the tanks ! "

Too late ! The torpedo crashed against our hull. This was
the end ; the detonation would blow us and our boat to pieces.
In a flash our thoughts turned to our loved ones at home and
we bade them a silent farewell. . . . But the expected explosion did not come . . . a dud ! We breathed again.

We dived to 40 metres and made off as fast as we could ; for
some time we heard the detonations of the depth-charges
which the enemy dropped all round the place where we had
disappeared. When we came to the surface about noon, the
sea was calm and deserted ; not a suspicious sign. We at

once wirelessed an exact description of our enemy to all the U-Boats cruising in the neighbourhood.

On May 1st the rugged solitary islands of St. Kilda rose out of the sea. We lay and sunned ourselves on deck for a few idle hours ; but some of us could not shake off the thought of yesterday. The bony hand of death had come too near.

In the afternoon I was sitting in the wireless cabinet with the head-phones over my ears, picking up the signals of enemy patrol-boats. The British Marconi stations were buzzing loudly. Familiar sounds suddenly rang in my ears ; a German U-Boat was calling, and I deciphered the message, which ran : " To all German U-Boats ; have just sunk U-Boat decoy with a double shot." She had gone to the bottom with every living soul on board. It was a pity that three torpedoes had been wasted on her. So her padded hull had not saved her, and her load of ammunition must have made her destruction more complete. I flung open the door of the wireless-room and shouted :

" Boys ! Another U-Boat has sunk that decoy ! "

And the boat shook with three resounding cheers.

A U-Boat trap was the most unpleasant object we could meet. I recall one that was encountered by another boat of our flotilla. She had fired at an apparently harmless steamer in the blockade-zone ; while the English crew were escaping in the lifeboats, the U-Boat came up to give the vessel its *coup de grâce*. Suddenly a woman appeared on deck with a baby in her arms and began to run up and down like one distracted ; she seemed to have been forgotten in the general excitement. The U-Boat came alongside, and two seamen were sent on board. Suddenly the woman appeared to take leave of her senses ; she flung the child on to the U-Boat's deck. Some of our men rushed to catch it before it fell overboard. But the bundle was not a baby ; it was a bomb— fortunately a dud, or the boat would have been blown to pieces. And the woman was a sailor in disguise. His treachery pronounced his own sentence. It is interesting to remember

M

that people called us " Boches " and " Huns," though they
knew quite well they could always rely on our humanity.

On the night of May 2nd-3rd we were passing through the
North Channel and trying to take advantage of the strong
current that runs through it. About midnight a fog began to
gather. The patrols had already sighted us and sent up
rockets ; but we hoisted the English flag and came through
unharmed. They probably took us for one of their own
U-Boats. Next day at nine o'clock in the morning we were
just entering the Irish Sea. Ahead of us was a large patrol-
boat ; however, we had to pass her.

" Full speed ahead ; stand by the gun ! "

The English vessel fled ; we would gladly have pursued,
but the Commander did not choose to waste our ammunition
on such as her. About noon we passed the Isle of Man and
thought of all our comrades there imprisoned. At five
o'clock we altered course for Liverpool ; we had scarcely
done so when an enemy periscope was sighted, and, soon after,
three torpedoes hissed across the water towards us. We
swung the boat round and watched them dash past. The
man who fired them deserved to be cashiered for trying to
torpedo a quickly handled German U-Boat, on a calm sea, in
the fourth year of the war ; he could hardly have thought that
our look-outs were asleep. To our great disgust they did not
venture an artillery fight.

Towards evening the fog grew thicker ; it began to rain,
and visibility was very bad. About eight o'clock the fast
Liverpool-Dublin mail steamer came in sight ; we chased her
under water, but she was too fast for us and disappeared into
the fog. It was a genuine pea-soup fog, so we dived and
continued our voyage in comfort beneath the surface.

All was peace—not a smoke-cloud, nor a movement ; we
drove steadily onward until the middle of the following day.
About two o'clock a slender grey vessel appeared on the
horizon. Our accumulator battery was nearly run down, so
we decided on an artillery attack. We opened fire with the

8·8, and then, as we drew nearer, with the 10·5. The steamer looked like a blockade-runner, and paid little attention to our fire ; her wireless repeatedly gave us our position. Finally she, too, opened fire. Then two three-funnelled destroyers dashed up, an airship appeared, and several seaplanes roared above our heads. There was nothing for it ; in spite of our depleted battery, we had to dive, followed by a parting fusillade of depth-charges and aeroplane bombs. The depth-charges, at least, were announced by the noise of the destroyers above our heads ; but the bombs took us utterly by surprise. Moreover, as the weather was fine, the airmen could see the U-Boat at a depth of 25 or 30 metres ; and it was, of course, very dangerous to come to the surface. We could also detect the presence of patrol-boats by our submarine listening apparatus, but we had no means of knowing when aeroplanes were about. Later in the afternoon we cautiously rose, but had to dive again at once. Then we stopped all the engines and lay on the sea-floor. We knew there was an airship overhead from the repeated discharge of " eggs," which more than once fell so near that our electric lights went out. At ten o'clock we again rose, but the airship was still there ; perhaps she had exhausted her supply of bombs.

The air inside the U-Boat had now grown very thick ; it had not been possible to ventilate her for twenty hours. Some bottled oxygen was released from time to time, and the electric fans were set running ; but this made little difference. Our nerves were gradually giving out, and we grew more and more sleepy. A lubricating oil-tank had sprung a leak as a result of the fusillade to which we had been subjected ; the strong current was driving us towards the sandy corner of Cardigan Bay, and there was a serious risk that, when it was light, the British airmen would be able to bombard us at their leisure.

At five minutes past ten we rose again ; this time, to our vast relief, we succeeded in getting out of Cardigan Bay and recharging our battery. We pursued our course under cover of the fog. Eleven o'clock. We were getting a torpedo into position in the fore part of the boat, and six men were busy over the ton weight of metal and machinery ; we had scarcely fitted the heavy war-head, when the order " Diving-stations ! " rang out. Several depth-charges crashed into the water. The torpedo slipped forward along her greased grooves and shot down the tube before we had been able to secure it properly. There were only five men to hold it, as the sixth was attending to the emergency ventilating valves. If we let it go, it would explode and blow up the boat.

We held on for dear life, until our arms quivered with the strain. No one came to help us, no one knew what we went through. Those minutes seemed endless. At last the boat was on an even keel, and in a few seconds the torpedo was slipped quietly into its place, and the tube door slammed. We were so shaken that we could hardly stand. At eleven o'clock we came to the surface ; how good those cigarettes tasted !

The calendar recorded May 8th. In the early hours of the morning we fell in with an elegant steamer of about 8,000 tons ; we remained on the surface and fired a torpedo into her boiler-room at a range of 300 metres. She broke in two amidships, her boilers exploded with a thunderous roar, and she sank like a stone in two minutes. The captain was picked up. He shook his head at everything he saw, and especially when a few dozen aeroplane bombs crashed into the water all round us. We never discovered his nationality. When we were below playing the concertina he sat and watched us with an expression of set horror on his face. But he was not long to enjoy his unaccustomed surroundings. On May 10th we succeeded in torpedoing a 10,000-ton Cardiff coal steamer, an obstinate creature who tried to ram us. Only a few survivors escaped in a lifeboat, and we sent our silent captain to keep them company. Did he still go on shaking his head ? We shall never know.

And then for home. The U 54 had been in commission for two years, and I had served on her continuously. We had gone through much in those two years, and defied many storms and many enemies. The anniversary had to be celebrated, and officers and men made ready for a solemn feast of rejoicing.

We were making our way down the Norwegian coast on a pleasant sunny afternoon, when we suddenly sighted a destroyer dashing towards us. We did a crash dive; nearly 2,000 gallons of water poured into the boat, and we plunged, at an angle of 30 degrees, to a depth of 89 metres. All the machinery stopped except the electric light. Compressed air was promptly let into the tanks. Up went the bow, down went the stern, and everything in the boat crashed; we shot upwards until our bows were actually out of water. A flange in the oil-engine had cracked; water was pouring in, and above us was the destroyer. At last we got the boat on to an even keel, and the guns were manned. But the destroyer proved to be Norwegian. We had been below for only fifteen minutes, but they had been fifteen minutes' agony. Such was our anniversary celebration.

The Norwegian boat escorted us for an hour or so in a friendly way. We hoisted the English flag, and the genial Norwegian sailors shouted in farewell : " Hip, hip, hip, hurrah, England !"

On May 18th we reached Kiel, and the following day we docked at Wilhelmshaven. We landed what remained of our ammunition ; then we took a most refreshing bath, and slept for twelve hours in a bed. Anyone who had disturbed that sleep would have met a speedy end. And then for leave and home.

19

THE SINKING OF THE *JUSTITIA*

By

Wireless Operator Haidt

On the early morning of July 10th, 1918, U 54 was slowly approaching the Norwegian three-mile limit in the neighbourhood of Bergen. The small 1,000-ton steamers laden with the indispensable pit-props for English and French coal mines, or iron ore from Sweden, or butter and eggs from Denmark, were often to be met with in these waters. It was not long before we sighted a fine steamer which we prepared to sink, in accordance with the provisions of prize law ; but three Norwegian torpedo-boats dashed up and protested that the ship could not be sunk as she was within the three-mile limit. There was nothing for it but to let her go.

On the 12th we were off Fair Isle, where the English had laid a large mine-field, under which we dived. A fight, even with a superior enemy, I find far preferable to a passage through a mine-field under water. It is a very unpleasant feeling when the boat grazes against the mooring cable of a mine, and death bumps and crashes against the hull. To pass the time, the Commander was playing the flute to us in the men's quarters, I was accompanying him on the concertina, and the boys were singing ; the atmosphere grew positively gay, and hardly one among us, old hands as we were, thought of the awful danger that lurked around us for five long hours.

On the 13th we were on the surface, making in a westerly direction at top speed. Schools of porpoises were playing round the ship, which we knew foretold a change in the weather.

There was nothing for it but to let her go.

Towards evening the sky grew overcast and something of a sea got up. Perhaps the weather was responsible for the fact that there was not an enemy in sight. Not until midday on the 15th, shortly after we had finished some necessary repairs to our compass, did we fall in with the first patrols, which chased us vainly until evening. At 2 a.m. a 13,000-ton ship hove in sight, and we at once prepared to attack ; but, as she was no doubt carrying valuable cargo, she steamed at such high speed that we found it hard to overtake her. At 2.55 came the order : " First and second tubes. . . . Fire ! " A double shot at 1,000 metres.

Two tremendous detonations followed, and the great ship began to sink. In a last defiance her bow reared up at almost right angles out of the water. Strange smouldering flames burst out of her ; we made off at top speed. Suddenly a column of fire and smoke shot up like an erupting volcano, and with a terrific explosion the entire ship was blown to pieces. A blaze and a flash, and then—nothing. The sea was scattered with falling fragments, and a vast tidal wave rose up and nearly engulfed us. We stood as though turned to stone, watching that tremendous drama of destruction.

At five o'clock in the afternoon we fell in with UB 126, and exchanged greetings and experiences. At eight o'clock three destroyers and a U-Boat decoy appeared on the scene and forced us to dive, pursued by twenty-five depth-charges of the newest brand. The shadows of the night grew darker, and flying clouds obscured the moon. However, in the next few days the weather cleared, and visibility was good.

Morning broke clear and sunny on July 20th, and we all felt very cheerful. Excellent fighting weather ! We were confident we should meet a fine large steamer in the North Channel.

" Smoke-cloud on the starboard bow," announced the look-out man suddenly.

" . . . Three . . . four . . . smoke-clouds."

All of us who had them, fetched binoculars. " Nine . . .

ten . . . eleven smoke-clouds . . . in the middle of the line a large steamer with three masts and two funnels."

The nearer we approached the enemy, the more clearly we could distinguish details. The group of ships recalled a swarm of ants. Nearly sixty patrol-boats, destroyers, U-Boat chasers, etc., and a small cruiser protected the colossus. At first, her size and the similarity of outline made the Commander take her for the *Vaterland*, which had been lying in New York harbour at the outbreak of war, and had now been put into commission again ; she was, in fact, the new English steamer *Justitia*. The Commander at once decided to attack. The thought that we must get her at any cost inspired every single member of the crew. The weather was unusually clear, with a slow ground-swell. The Commander manœuvred his boat into position against the sun, so as to remain undiscovered as long as possible.

The giant suddenly altered course by 20 degrees and we were now on the wrong side of her. We had to swing round and dive under the leading escort vessels, which were madly scouring the sea. They had already discovered us, and were dashing about furiously above our heads ; a positive bombardment of sixty depth-charges forced us down to 50 metres. But the Commander would not be deterred from his decision to attack. We came up to periscope-depth. Two depth-charge explosions underneath us forced—nay, flung—us to the surface.

There was the giant, now just within range, and between us and her a large destroyer bearing down on us at full speed. She tried to ram us, but the Commander was too quick for her.

" First and second tubes—fire ! "

" Dive at full speed."

The boat dipped steeply : all about us was the crash of explosions ; we were not moving, we were falling. If we did not reach the desired depth soon, it would be all up with us.

We lay at a depth of 59 metres.

Two tremendous detonations announced that our bronze

fish had done their work bravely and well. A dwarf had brought down a giant.

But we had no time for rejoicing. The lights went out. Pocket torches were produced, and frantic efforts were made to turn on the emergency lighting. The boat was so tilted forward that it almost stood on end ; we all scrambled up the stern to try to redress the balance. We could not stand up ; we clutched at the iron plates and tore our finger-nails. It seemed almost impossible to get the boat on to an even keel. But the thought of home, that we wanted—nay, were determined—to see again, endowed us with superhuman strength.

At last ! We had succeeded. God be thanked, for He had helped us. Our nerves grew calmer. But danger was not past. The exploding depth-charges announced that the enemy was hard at our heels ; the engines were stopped, and we were ordered to keep absolutely quiet.

Fortunately there was a strong current, and our leaky oil-tank could not betray us. The depth-charges were already falling a little further off.

The incoming water made the air worse and worse every minute. Four times we tried to come up, but the enemy forced us below again. At our fourth appearance the air-pressure shot our Commander like a ball through the conning-tower hatch. He almost fell overboard. At six o'clock the Chief Engineer reported that we could only dive once more ; the current in the electric battery would then be exhausted. The Commander's responsibility was heavy, and he decided to come up to the surface at once.

Scarcely was the conning-tower above water than the hatch was flung open, and the gun-crews dashed to their weapons. In a few moments both were ready for action. No ship was in the immediate neighbourhood, but all around us was a circle of ships on the look-out. Surely, however, there was a small gap in the southern corner ? There was !

" Full speed ahead ; charge batteries ; ventilate ship ! "

We were not yet discovered. The gunners stood tense at

their posts ; they had plenty of ammunition, and the guns were ready to fire. Almost 100 yards from the gap in the line the enemy sighted us, and guns began to thud and flash. The effect on us was one of extreme relief. Now we could act. Orders were given to fire, and we began to enjoy life again, unfortunately for the nearest patrol-boat. Our gunners were magnificent. In five short minutes she was sinking ; and the others that came to her rescue soon met the same fate.

We had broken through. We could dive once more, and not an enemy could see us.

Next morning we fell in with UB 64 : she came alongside, and we gave her a spare wireless amplifier. The UB 64 reported with great satisfaction that one of our torpedoes had blown up the engine-room of the destroyer which had tried to ram us. They also told us that the *Justitia*—we now learnt the name of our gigantic enemy—had capsized and sunk three hours after the attack. The UB 64 had, in fact, fired a torpedo at her a few days before, and she was turning back to go into dock for repair, when we gave her the death-blow.

In the course of the next few days we were able to add a troop-transport to our list of victims ; but in this encounter we suffered a good deal of damage, and were compelled to make straight for home. In due course we hailed with delight the island of Heligoland as it rose slowly out of the waves in the reddish glow of the setting sun. Home !

Soon after, we docked at Wilhelmshaven to the strains of the band of H.M.S. *Hamburg*. The Emperor came on board and shook hands with every member of the crew. When warned of the greasy state of the engine controls, he said :

" What is good enough for my sailors is good enough for me."

If the Emperor had come to see us oftener, much might have been avoided. Few people at home understood the men on active service.

20

FROM TRAINING-SHIP TO THE HIGH SEAS

By

Boatswain's Mate Seidel

OUR ship was lying in Flensburg harbour. It had been the scene of busy activity until the day before ; all the preparations, great and small, were being made for a new training-voyage. And to-day war had been declared. What would be done with boys like ourselves ? We were still under age—most of us between fifteen and seventeen. After a long wait we were told that anyone who liked could go ; but those who got permission from their homes could stay. With much effort I managed to persuade my parents and was allowed to stay.

Our education was vigorously taken in hand : seamanship, infantry and gun-drill, and signalling, followed in rapid succession. I liked signalling best. However, the weeks of training went quicker than we thought, and we began to wonder where we should be ordered to report. My last day of signal-instruction proved decisive. I was in luck, and saw my long-cherished wish come to fulfilment : I was posted for airship service. But my joy was not to last long, for an order came in that the best signallers were to be assigned to U-K. U-K is the submarine department. It was the exactly opposite of what I wanted. However, if I could not get above the enemy, I would get beneath him, and I resigned myself.

More training at Kiel ; no light matter, as I was soon to realise. I had to keep most uncommonly wide awake. A submarine is a very complicated apparatus, full of names and designations of instruments whose purpose I did not so much as suspect. The theory was the worst part ; I got on much more quickly with the practical side, and very soon understood the working of a U-Boat. Day and night we learned and laboured ; we wanted to get at the enemy as quickly as we could.

" Imagine a steel cylinder," our Petty-Officer used to say, " terminating in a point at either end. In the centre of it on the upper side is a tower. Aft—that is, at the back end— there are two torpedo-tubes on the under side. Next to them is the electric kitchen, then the electric motors, and then the Diesel engine-room. Then the control-room, with the compass, the horizontal rudder-wheel, and the valves. In front of that is the officers' and warrant officers' room. Right in front, in the bow, are two more torpedo-tubes. Between every compartment is a bulkhead, and a hatchway leads from the conning-tower to the body of the vessel. The control-room is the most important part of the boat—as, indeed, its name implies. The periscopes are in the conning-tower. Built against the exterior of the boat are the diving-tanks which give the boat its shape. To them are attached the horizontal rudders, two on each side, one in front and one behind."

The Petty-Officer made this all clear to us by means of models, and we soon grasped it. The instruction proceeded :

" In front of the conning-tower is the gun ; and the two hawsers that run from bow to stern over the conning-tower serve as some sort of protection against mines. Between them are the wireless antennæ."

For weeks every detail was so impressed upon our minds that we knew it all. The day for the first practice-voyage was already fixed, when an order came in that we were to prepare to join the U-Boat flotilla in the Adriatic.

Twelve strong, our little company travelled across Germany and Austria, stopping for a few hours in both Berlin and Vienna, visits which we greatly enjoyed. In Pola we were posted to our various boats ; my boat lay at Cattaro. An

Austrian torpedo-boat conveyed me down the lovely Dalma-
tian coast to my destination ; and as soon as I arrived, I at
once reported on board. The boat had just returned from a
voyage ; she was being energetically refitted for her next
trip, and I was set very heartily to work with the rest. The
various motors had to be cleaned, the diving-tanks tested, the
fresh-water tank scoured, and the boat repainted inside and
out. Fourteen days' ceaseless work. I ceased to be conscious
of time ; but all this was very little to my taste. I wanted to
start on my first trip under water. The others comforted me
and said I should not have to wait long.

We had nearly finished. Tank-ships came alongside ; we
took in fuel for the Diesel engines, and drinking water, and
there were certain preliminaries to a voyage that were never
neglected. Under-water tests were carried out to ensure that
the boat would lie on an even keel. I was getting quite familiar
with my work. " Cast off ! " came the order. I was at the
wheel. A steamer accompanied us to protect us from being
attacked or rammed. We were now ordered below, and the
Commander shut the conning-tower hatch. I was in a state
of high excitement, as I had never yet been under water.
Then followed the order to flood the tanks, put the aft rudders
up and the bow rudders down. A hiss of rushing water and
the boat sank to 20 metres. The engineer and the technical
personnel examined every detail, for the lives of all of us
depend on the proper functioning of the boat in every particular. Various further tests were carried out, and then the
order came to break surface. The depth rudders were
put over and the boat gradually moved upwards. The upper
valves of the diving-tanks were closed. Compressed air
hissed into the tanks and forced the water through the now
open valves on the under side, and the boat appeared once
more on the surface. Again we dived. A torpedo-tube was
flooded—that is, the tube was filled with water, the ends of it
being closed with steel doors. The outer door was opened,
and a charge of compressed air was fired, to ascertain the

effect of the shot upon the boat. Again we emerged and made fast to the pier. Our work was over for the day.

Early on the following day provisions were taken on board, and finally the ammunition. Eight torpedoes disappeared through the fore hatch, and two through the after hatch. Four of them were fitted with war-heads and thrust into the tubes ; the other four were stored under the lowest bunks, two on each side of the boat. This difficult work needed the greatest care. About 400 shells for our gun were taken in, as well as ammunition for the machine-gun and pistols. Last of all the bombs were put on board.

After much exertion and anxiety everything was at last in order, we carried out another test dive, and at last were ready for sea. A brief exchange of chaff with our comrades on our mother-ship, moored close beside us, and the order " Cast off ! " rang out ; the Diesel engines started with a roar, and we moved at half speed towards the harbour entrance. Austrian torpedo-boats accompanied us through the mine-fields, and then we were alone. I was at the wheel, and this was my first watch on my first submarine voyage. It was misty, and a cold wind blew from starboard. Shadows appeared in front of us—the enemy. We dived, and the Otranto barrage lay behind us.

The beauty and majesty of the sea affected me deeply ; but I had no time for dreams. The wheel demanded my whole attention. I had until now felt perfectly well, but the boat began to pitch and roll, and Neptune claimed his first victim. The air below became more and more oily and thick. If only the water would grow a little calmer !

Two days later several steamers came into sight. We were all full of eagerness and enthusiasm ; a single will inspired us all, a single thought held us and made us labour like one man. The first and second torpedo-tubes were flooded, and the outer caps opened. The engine telegraph clanged, and orders were shouted down to the man at the wheel. Moments of tense excitement followed as we steamed forward to attack. " First tube ready—fire ! " The boat shook, the torpedo was off. Once more the order, and a second torpedo was on its way. Deathlike silence in the boat . . . and then a distant crash. Both shots had hit. We looked at each other with glad faces as the order came for a crash dive. Enemy destroyers were already on the look-out for us. We dropped quickly beneath the surface ; I counted 30 . . . 35 metres. A violent explosion, the boat quivered, and all the lights went out. The emergency lighting was turned on. Then followed a series of detonations—depth-charges ; very unpleasant things for the novice, but one soon got used to them. After an attack the boat has to travel at half speed on the surface to recharge her batteries.

Many encounters followed, varied by an occasional successful artillery duel. In many cases we sent a party on board to blow up the captured ship. Later on, when merchant-ships were also armed, we had to fight, but we almost always won. Many and triumphant were our voyages, and we could boast of many sunken ships ; we gradually began to pride ourselves on our success. We were utterly convinced that we should win the war : how grievously we were deceived !

At the beginning of October, 1918, we were returning from a long voyage. In Cattaro, as usual, the boat was overhauled and refitted. This time we were to leave Cattaro for the last time. Austria-Hungary had collapsed, and the enemy was at the gates. Were we to surrender our boat to the enemy ? That was not to be thought of ; but we could not try to get away, for no oil was to be had. So we prepared the torpedoes and set the fuses of the bombs. The boat was brought into the centre of the harbour, and the fuses were released.

Hurriedly we left our beloved vessel and got into a motor-boat. The pennon streamed in the breeze. A detonation, and the U-Boat had vanished. Tears came into the eyes of the Commander, and of many of the crew, as we saw the end of the boat which had preserved us against so many perils. The other boats in the Cattaro flotilla, together with the torpedo and mine ship, were blown up at the same time. Nothing fell into the enemy's hands.

Successful artillery attack ; the crew leaving a burning steamer.

We had many difficulties to encounter, not to mention actual fights with sundry Slovenes, before we made our way home.

21

FROM KIEL TO CATTARO

By

Wireless Operator Ruhland

At last, after weeks of brief trips in Kiel Bay, our crew was now welded into an effective human organism, and we were ready to start our voyage into the blue Mediterranean. Day after day we had awaited our orders ; now they had come. The crew, drawn up on deck, listened to a heartening address from the head of the Submarine Department ; then the order rang out : " Cast off ! " and with three cheers we put out to sea, sped on our way by the cheerful strains of a band. The members of the crew not on duty stayed on deck to watch the slowly dimming horizon ; for a long while the wind carried to their ears the sounds of their native land until these gradually died away.

The boat steamed through the gentle swell of the Baltic, on its way to the Sound. We stopped, as we fell in with a cruiser that was patrolling the Sound, and we spent a last few hours in cheerful company. Then we finally bade farewell to home. We passed through the Sound during the night, and the North Sea soon greeted us with bad weather and a heavy sea. The first victims of sea-sickness went down : one young man from Cologne, the torpedo-hand, was sadly reduced, and had to reserve a basin for his own permanent use. The strongly patrolled Dover-Calais barrage prevented us taking the nearest route through the Channel. So we steered for the Orkneys and thence pursued our peaceful course round England ; the voyage was quite uneventful as the result of the far-flung activity of our U-Boats. Not a ship came in sight the whole time.

At last, off the mouth of the Channel, the look-out shouted : " Sailing-ship in sight." She should be the first on the list of ships sunk by us during the voyage. She stopped, her boat was soon alongside, and a cheerful, rather stout old sea-dog, who found it hard to squeeze through the conning-tower hatch, came to take up his abode in our fo'castle. He was obviously in terror, and believed that the " Boches " would twist his neck. His papers showed that his ship was the American sailing-ship *Will H. Clifford*, 1,600 tons, bound for New York. We planted a few shells in her and soon set her on fire. Soon the friendly line of the Biscay coast came into view ; we rounded Cape Finisterre, drew nearer inshore and set a course for Lisbon. On this long voyage we did not espy a single victim ; we were damned to inactivity, as the boredom on our faces showed. It was not until an English boat crossed our course that our hearts beat higher, and we set to work at once. She was a fine deep-sea tug, with a barge in tow laden with ice-machines. We felt almost sorry to disturb the crew at their supper ; but war is war. The tug was quickly sunk, sixteen men of its crew were sent in the lifeboat to Spain, and the remaining four were squeezed into our U-Boat.

On the following day we did great execution in Lisbon waters. A number of sailing-vessels, mostly laden with cork or wheat, were sent to the bottom by our torpedoes, until a hooting of a siren on the heights above the city showed us that our activity had been observed. An ancient Portuguese ship-of-war put out to sea at once ; she observed us dubiously, looked us up and down—and promptly took to flight. She dashed off at such a speed that we were unable to catch her up and give her something to remember us by.

We then made for Gibraltar. On our way, a very satis-factory haul unfortunately slipped through our fingers. The crews of three steamers had already taken to their boats, when a British destroyer suddenly appeared on the scene, and forced us to leave our prey and seek deeper regions. As some measure of compensation, four hours later we fell in with a Portuguese sailing-ship with a cargo of iron ore ; this time we sunk the ship by explosive cartridges. The neighbourhood of Gibraltar was to be a very profitable one : we fired torpedo after torpedo, and our list of victims was considerably lengthened ; it included two English steamers and a vessel that had once been Austrian.

In the Mediterranean.

Our lubricating oil showed signs of giving out, and compelled us to leave these waters and make the best of our way to our destination. We passed Gibraltar by night and unobserved, and the following morning revealed to us all the beauty of the Mediterranean Sea : calm and azure-blue, and glittering in the golden sunshine. How delightful it would have been to visit these lovely shores on a pleasure trip ! But our boat was everything but comfortable. The water even was rationed, so that it was not possible to shave : both officers and men were growing wild and woolly beards. Faces and hands had

A few shells soon set the sailing-ship on fire.

gradually grown so black that not a patch of bright skin was visible. Sometimes one or other of us did make an effort to scrape the deposit of dirt off with the help of sea-water, but without success. But in spite of these disabilities we were in a cheerful mood. Our success hitherto and the prospect of further activities made our deprivations easy to bear.

The day was drawing to a close when we reached the Algiers - Marseilles steamer - route. A brightly - lit steamer passed across our course. We were soon in position : noise-lessly the torpedo sped on its way, and a mighty detonation announced a hit. Another victim—English also ; she, too, quickly disappeared beneath the waves. Two Greeks whom we fished out of the water were accommodated with their allies. Next morning it became obvious that the two new-comers were accompanied by a certain breed of small insects, and, to their great indignation, we compelled them to shear each other's long manes.

We caught an Italian three-masted sailing-ship just entering the Ionian Sea and compelled her to alter her course to the bottom. This last victim raised our total of sunk tonnage to 21,000.

We had now to concentrate on getting unmolested to our destination. We had to keep a sharp look-out, manœuvre the ship with the utmost care, if we were not to fall a victim to one of the numerous patrols that were cruising day and night in the Straits of Otranto. We were soon past the danger-zone, and in the proud consciousness of having served the Father-land and damaged the enemy we made our way into Cattaro Bay. When we landed, I had every right to regard myself as an experienced U-Boat seaman.

22

RAID ON THE SARDINIAN PORT OF CARLOFORTE (S. PIETRO ISLAND)

By

Boatswain's Mate Seidel

WE were splashing gaily about in the clear blue waters that wash the rocky shores of Cattaro. It was real April weather, a day of southern sunshine and deep blue sky. Two new arrivals, with whom we had been disporting ourselves in the sea, had brought a little variety into our time of idleness. They were wireless men who were to make themselves useful to us on our longer voyages ; but they had yet to prove their capacity.

The lovely day soon drew to an end, and vigorous preparations began for our next voyage.

In a pitch-black night we slipped out of the Bocche, led by two Austrian destroyers with their mine-sweep out. The red steering-light at the stern of each destroyer served as our only guiding point of direction in the sinister darkness. We reached Punta d'Ostra, at the egress to the bay, without hindrance. The destroyers signalled good luck and returned to port. Once more, for several weeks, we were left to our own resources.

We pursued our way briskly to the Straits of Otranto, which were unceasingly watched by a swarm of enemy patrol-boats, and blocked by several U-Boat nets. A patrol forced us to dive, and soon afterward a U-Boat net forced us up again, and it was with feelings of something like despair that we came up to the surface. I clambered at once into the conning-tower and observed that we were indeed encircled by patrols. Only the impenetrable darkness and our own skilful manœuvring saved us. Scarcely had we got about 100 metres beyond the boom, than a rocket soared up hissing and spitting into the sky. We were discovered. Then followed a tumult of explosions. By diving at full speed to 50 metres we escaped the menace of the depth-charges. Our visitors, who were unused to such a hectic life, were utterly dumbfounded.

For several days we scoured the sea, but saw nothing suspicious. We grew bored ; day in, day out, nothing but the sky and sea over and about us. Our wireless friends sat at their apparatus, intently listening ; not a sound. We stood and strained our eyes into the distance. Suddenly our friends' faces lit up ; they burst into a shout of delight and rushed to the Commander with the news :

" A convoy making for Sardinia."

Were these fellows to beat us at our own game ? Intolerable ! However, in spite of doubts as to their reliability, we laid a course for Sardinia.

They were right ; there was the convoy, steaming peacefully along in the bright moonlight. We could not let such a chance escape, and attacked at once. A few minutes later the first and second ships had heeled over, and the third took to flight. But our wireless friends were obstinate and would not let her go. They soon located her, and just as dawn was breaking we had overtaken her—a tank steamer with one gun.

The Commander decided on attack by gunfire, and we were all glad to think that " Auntie " up on deck should have a chance of making herself heard. She soon tore a hole in the enemy's hull, from which heavy oil poured out in streams ; but the ship showed no signs of surrender. It was not until a shot exploded her ammunition supply that she was silent. A sheet of flame enveloped her, and her gallant crew went with her to the bottom.

A patrol-boat appeared, and forced us to dive ; her, too, we sank with a well-aimed torpedo.

Our rising war-barometer suddenly stopped, however, when our wireless operators picked up a message to the effect that the two ships we had torpedoed first were not sunk, but had slipped into harbour at Carloforte, at the southernmost point of Sardinia.

What should we do ? The place was not far away, and we decided to pay it a visit. The day was fine and sunny, and we were soon lying off the harbour mouth ; we dived, raised the periscope, and inspected our position. At first we were at a loss how to get into the harbour, but towards evening a coasting steamer kindly showed us the way through the somewhat circuitous approach. We waited until darkness began to fall, then rose to the surface, carried up ammunition for the gun, and cleared the decks for action. About midnight we made our way into the harbour. I was one of the gun's-crew and could observe the town and harbour lights at my leisure. The inhabitants were asleep, and no one could have suspected our presence. Our prey, a fine 10,000-ton steamer, lay moored to the quay, and near by were two deep-sea tugs and several sailing-boats. It was too dark to take the offensive, so we slipped out of the harbour once more and reappeared at dawn. We made straight at the great steamer, and in few seconds a torpedo struck her amidships ; she broke in two with a crash, and both parts sank vertically to the bottom. The two tugs beside her had vanished.

The tremendous detonation must have rudely awakened many of the inhabitants from their morning slumbers ; and they were no doubt anxiously asking each other what could have been the cause of this thunderous uproar. We were not disposed to leave them long in doubt. We dropped a few shells on to the harbour works, and then set the sailing-vessels on fire by some well-directed shots. It was an odd feeling calmly to be sinking ships in the middle of an enemy harbour.

The Italians had not reckoned on so bold and romantic a foray. It was not until some little while had passed, when we had already done a good deal of damage, that a motor-boat dashed out, circled round some anchored tugs, and opened a brisk fire with a small gun. We manœuvred on a zig-zag course, flung a few shells at the little reptile, and frightened her home again. Then the coast batteries began to come into action ; heavy stuff crashed into the water near our bows and screamed over our decks. Things were growing too hot for us. Guns were sputtering and roaring from every side and corner. After a couple more shots at the motor-boat, we swung our gun round and made off with all the engines running at full speed. At last we reached deeper water where we could dive ; but suddenly there came a report from the engine-room : " Motor out of action ! " This was the last straw. Our hearts stood still. After some minutes of awful suspense, we were all ordered forward and the boat slowly sank. Meantime our wireless friends had picked up the message : " German U-Boat sunk in harbour." By way of indicating that we were still afloat we deposited a couple of morning salutations, in the form of shells, into the wireless station, which was clearly visible.

However, it was high time to make ourselves scarce. Two armed trawlers were now attacking us astern. We swung our gun round and replied ; when we had dropped a visiting-card on the first trawler's deck, a whirr and a roar in the air above us compelled us to dive. Aeroplanes were circling over us and steadily dropping bombs ; while the thud of propellers betrayed the presence of several destroyers.

We dared not show ourselves ; we waited until darkness fell, and then cautiously raised our periscope. Although there were enemy ships in every direction, the Commander decided to come up, and we escaped in safety.

On our way home we sighted one more solitary steamer. As she was moving at high speed on a zig-zag course, she was difficult to overtake, but we finally succeeded in putting our last torpedo into her. Near the Straits of Otranto we exchanged greetings with an outgoing German U-Boat. They were to be the last that her crew were destined to receive ; that U-Boat never returned. We reached the straits in heavy weather and passed through them unmolested. Our friends and allies in Cattaro harbour gave us the heartiest reception ; but what we liked most to think of was our gay and gallant foray into the Port of Carloforte.

23

AIR ATTACK

By
Boatswain's Mate Seidel

AFTER a successful five weeks' voyage we were making our way into Cattaro harbour, escorted by an Austrian torpedo-boat destroyer. Here, the Adriatic has eaten deeply into the land like a Norwegian fjord, forming three picturesque inlets on the way. The dark mountains, crowned by rock-hewn fortifications, fall steep and sheer into the sea. At the far end of the gulf lies the main fortress of Cattaro, protected by Nature against any surprise attack.

Above the town and gulf of Cattaro the sky was bright and cloudless—just the weather for lounging, bathing, and sleeping while our beloved U-Boat was being refitted and repaired. We sat outside the barracks where we were quartered during our stay in port, and passed the day in various idle pursuits.

" Proper flying weather to-day," said one man with a laugh.

Scarcely had he uttered the words, when a whirr and a roar above us broke the stillness, and—a cloud of dust and vapour shot up into the air.

Bombs !

It was some while before the Austrian siren-alarm was sounded, but by that time it was superfluous, as we had already received the Italians' visiting-card.

We peered out of our bomb-proof dug-outs looking for these whirring, roaring birds, but could not see them. Where were they ? Suddenly a body of Austrians dashed round the corner of the barracks, white with dust from top to toe ; they explained that a bomb had exploded in a lime quarry just as they were passing it. We congratulated them on their escape, and chaffed them on their appearance.

Tac-tac-tac-tac-tac-tac . . .

Suspecting that this was the rattle of Italian machine-guns, we hurried down to the quay-side.

"Four . . . Five . . . Ten . . . over there. . . . Can't you see them ? "

" Eleven . . . Fifteen . . . Eighteen . . . Twenty-four. . . ."

Tac-tac-tac-tac . . .

" Take cover ! "

But we could not bear to stay in our shelters ; we rushed to our boat, dragged out the heavy machine-gun, and joined in the fight.

Three . . . four bombs crashed into the water round our boat, but none hit her ; we wrenched at the machine-gun lever—tac-tac-tac . . .

A general cannonade soon started ; guns of every kind and calibre cracked and boomed, and the concerted bombardment gradually swelled into a hellish din. The Italians began to feel uncomfortable, and one airman after another circled higher and higher into the sky. Like tiny black specks, they vanished into the west ; the white puffs of smoke dispersed and the guns fell silent.

This unwelcome visit had one excellent result—a rich and various haul of fish, stunned and driven ashore by the bombs that fell into the sea. They were busily collected by Austrian sailors and prisoners of war when the attack was over.

We felt extremely empty, but had to bear up for a while, as a stray bomb had blown up our dinner. This time the joke was with the Austrians.

24

IN EASTERN WATERS

By

Leading Seaman A. Unterleitner

WILHELMSHAVEN. One day in July, 1918, I stood before my Divisional Officer on the deck of a battleship of the first squadron, absorbed in a recollection of the five years I had served aboard her ; joys and sorrows, distress and deprivation, memories of many voyages and encounters of the war, Skagerrak and Ösel, raced through my head. All that was over. War in the air and war beneath the sea demanded many victims, and reinforcements had to be found in the High Sea Fleet. And now I was marked down for what had come to be known as a voyage to the next world.

"Come now, make up your mind, my dear Unterleitner ; we need a reliable range-taker for Z 72—the air is just as important as the sea these days."

"If you please, Sir, would you kindly support my transfer to UK 139 ? " I answered. " I've been trying to get seconded to the U-Boat Flotilla for the last two years."

"What ! . . . But how do you know they want you on the new U-Cruiser ? You don't ask much, do you ? "

"I think you'll find it's all right, Sir. I asked Lieutenant W—— to apply for me, and he made sure about it."

Lieutenant W—— had been on our ship, and at that moment was Torpedo Officer on the famous U-Cruiser. After a brief pause while I contemplated the plates and rivets on the cabin ceiling, the Divisional Officer reappeared with the Commander whom he had gone to consult, and handed me an order for medical examination in the sick-bay. An hour later I brought back a certificate of fitness for U-Boat service.

"Very well; helm hard a-starboard, and good luck. You'll get your orders to-morrow."

There I stood, glad, and yet a little dashed, that everything had gone so quickly after two years of waiting. Walking like a man holding up a wetted finger to catch the direction of the wind, I went back to my quarters in a kind of dull oppression. I hoped the ship would forgive me for deserting her ; for five years she had been my home, and I should always think of her with loyal affection. Morning came. Black as crows, we stood in the coal barge alongside the ship, oozing with sweat, wielding our shovels, while above us swung the tipping baskets laden with precious black mineral that other sailors, black as laughing niggers, lowered to its destination in the bunkers, to the cheerful strains of the ship's band. I was gazing upward, keeping a sharp look-out on the movements of a large jar of lemonade, when suddenly among those niggers appeared the white face of an orderly :

" Hi ! Luis, you've got to get out of that ; here's something for you."

He grinned amiably, and flung me an official envelope.

I felt dizzy and had to sit down for a moment or two. Then I said good-bye to all my friends, reported to the Petty-Officer on duty, and stepped into the bathroom to wash the dirt off a " Heligolander," young in years but old in seafaring. The hour of departure was really at hand. Once more I had to report to the Divisional Officer and the Commander. I was given a small package secured by a green and white band, containing my service-medal, pay, rations, and travelling warrant to Kiel. Then the post-launch came alongside, and with that departing sailor and his bundle went a small fragment of the life of H.M.S. ——. He watched her for a long while until her silhouette vanished in the mist. . . . I felt as though I were homeless, and I was not ashamed of the tears that came into my eyes.

Kiel.   Nearly five years before, on my way round Skagen to take my service-oath at Kiel, I had had my first experience of life on the great waters.   Once again I stood on the narrow quay beside the harbour.   From across the water came all the conflicting noises of a repair-yard : yonder was a long grey object in the water anchored near the docks ; beneath me lay a small dinghy in which sat a sailor in leather overalls.   When I had waited for half an hour and still did not know how I was to get across, I plucked up courage and shouted to the man in the dinghy :

"Hullo, young fellow ! "

To which he replied :   " Hullo, my lad ! "

"What sort of boat's that over there ? "

" A U-Boat."

" I can see that for myself."

He looked at me with meditative suspicion ; then it suddenly came over him that I must be the man whom he was to meet, and with a soft whistle he proceeded :

" Well, I'll pull you over, if you're the lad I'm waiting for."

And so the lad was rowed across and greeted with a hearty cheer from the crew, who happened to be off duty at the moment.   After reporting myself, I went below into the interior of that terror of the seas.   My luck was in, for a week later the Zeppelin to which I was to have been transferred was shot down over England.

Work began at once.   We were under orders for the Eastern Baltic.   We stood in an ammunition barge and loaded shells for our two 15 cm. guns, while the torpedo ratings stowed away their treasures in the bows.   My friend of the jolly-boat, whose name proved to be Hermann, got in everyone's way, scrawled on the shells with chalk, cracked dirty jokes, and succeeded in making us all laugh in spite of our exhaustion. The First Lieutenant, a very genial fellow, who treated us all as his family, bore a hand, and everything was soon in order. When we had taken in fuel, water, and supplies, we cast off for our first long voyage.   We were to patrol Russian waters, a task of no small difficulty and peril owing to the numerous shallows and mine-fields.

We started at night. Softly and in utter silence we slipped out of the Kiel estuary and made for the open sea, where we were to cruise and keep watch. The waves hissed past our hull as we sped into the gathering dawn. The sun rose like a ball of fire, in a blaze of brilliant colour. The fresh breeze was as exhilarating as a plunge. We filled our lungs

The waves hissed past our hull as we sped into the gathering dawn.

with the keen salt air, and in silent wonder contemplated the marvellous spectacle of the sunrise. How small was man against that tremendous waste of waters ! All about us seemed so still and peaceful, and yet we were a ship-of-war hunting for our enemies. Not a sign or a movement on the horizon. We fell in with but one small vessel flying the German flag, and after an exchange of signals she made off homewards.

Towards evening, I suddenly descried a small black speck on the horizon which grew gradually larger. I tried to estimate the distance ; in so doing, I observed four other small specks disengage themselves in rapid succession from the one in front, and I made my report.

" Smoke-clouds five points to port, probably torpedo-boats " ; but I could not yet give the range.

" Right," said the Commander.   " Crew to diving-stations ; range-taker to remain."

We were more or less off Danzig, and we had therefore to discover whether these were friends or foes.   All binoculars were fixed on the five tiny plumes of smoke.   They made a short turn to the left, and we could see the curves of foam at their bows as they bore down on us in echelon formation.

" Range-taker report."

" . . . 9,000 metres . . . 8,400 metres . . . 7,000 metres. . . .   Flag-signals on leading boat, but not the signal for opening fire."

The Commander stood with his eyes steadily fixed on the five dark objects.   They were now within 5,000 metres of us, and suddenly made a quarter-turn to the left, so that they were now moving right across our course.   They were German boats, a German half-flotilla.   It was not long before the leading vessel was within hail ; we exchanged news, and it transpired that they were patrol-boats in charge of a mine-laying flotilla and were now bound for Danzig to provision and get a few days' rest.   We sped eastward, and were soon alone and desolate in the stillness of the night ; only the moon looked down on us and scattered her silver radiance over the waste of waters.

*   *   *   *   *

For six hours we had been lying in Danzig harbour alongside another U-Boat, a somewhat smaller sister.   After a brief spell ashore, and refuelling, we put to sea again to test the boat's diving capacity off Danzig, escorted by two destroyers. Once more—sea and sky, sky and sea.   So desolate and yet so lovely.   A light breeze ruffled the deep blue water.

" Get ready to dive ! "

The two T-Boats were signalled to stand by. Our new U-Cruiser was now to show whether she was well and truly clinched and riveted, whether she was equal to all demands that might be made upon her at great depths—whether, in a word, she could live up to her proud name.

" Diving-stations ! "

Wireless masts and guns were lashed in position, and everything on deck made ready for diving. The hatches were clamped down and the valves closed ; the boat was cleared for action. Orders came by telephone and speaking-tube to the fore and aft compartments, to the control-room, and the engine-room. The periscopes were lowered, the compressed air blown out of the tanks, which were quickly filled with water. The boat slid slowly downwards. . . . There was a buzzing in my ears, and my breath stuck in my throat ; my brain ceased to function, for a few moments my body seemed on the verge of collapse, and then . . . suddenly all was well. The will had resumed control. Deeper and deeper we sank, until we were 40 metres under water. At that point the boat seemed to get out of control, or possibly the ground swell interrupted her progress. We crowded forward through the narrow manholes so as to depress the bow, and, by judicious flooding and distribution of weight, soon got the boat in hand once more. We sank and sank, deeper and deeper. . . .

Suddenly a sharp shock was felt ; we listened. The vessel was now 90 metres below the surface ; she seemed to be labouring in agony, moisture was soaking through the deck and trickling down the sides of the hull, we all shivered with sudden alternations of heat and cold ; then another shock, as though something had been wrenched off the hull. With clenched teeth every man laboured at his post, half unconscious, mechanically carrying out his orders. All who were not actively engaged rushed fore or aft, as might be needed, to keep the boat on an even keel.

Slowly, very slowly, the heavy boat moved upwards. 50

. . . 30 . . . 15 metres ; the periscopes were raised. The
Commander peered cautiously round the boat. Two black
objects could be seen floating alongside—could they be mines ?
The two destroyers observed them as they gurgled towards the
surface. Our decks were now clear and the hatches were
opened. The two mysterious objects bobbed up beside us
and proved on nearer inspection to be our telephone-buoys,
that had become detached owing to the pressure of the water
and had floated upwards. The attachments were intact, and
all was soon in order once again. After a short talk with
the two destroyers they turned and made for home ; we laid
a course eastward.

It is always melancholy when, after a long or short association, friends and ships separate in waters where the enemy is
lurking, or from which he is not very far away, to go upon their
various purposes. Alone, utterly self-dependent, the little
ship that carries death, and is itself beset by death, pursues her
way, and on this mighty element God seems very powerful
and very near.

To starboard, we were slowly approaching a long dark line
on the horizon. We thought we heard a distant thudding and
rumbling like the sound of heavy guns ; or was it an illusion ?
The dark line to starboard has materialised into a lovely
wooded coast edged by stretches of white sand and strips of
sunlit meadow, and dotted with a few peasants' or fishermen's
huts : a truly Russian scene.

The boat suddenly stopped ; three small vessels appeared
ahead of us as though they had risen out of the sea. Their
white transparent smoke betrayed the use of oil fuel. Were
they enemy mine-sweepers or harmless trawlers ? We, also, and
our guns, manned and ready for action, had not escaped their
notice. They were moving slowly ; we had come upon them
just as they were putting out to sea. They apparently ignored
our signal to stop ; but a shell across their bows made them
take notice. However, they showed no signs of heaving-to,
and, indeed, they appeared to be making off at full speed,

when suddenly there came a spurt of flame from the leading ship. She was shooting with a small calibre gun. The shot fell short and to the left ; we turned, drew off a little, and then opened a furious fire with our stern gun. The fourth shell scored a hit, and the fifth set the leading boat on fire. The two others did not shoot, being apparently unarmed. We concentrated on the leader, and at the third salvo a cloud of dust and wreckage shot up into the air ; a minute later her place was empty, and only some drifting timbers marked a sailors' icy grave. The list of Russian auxiliary vessels was shorter by one U-Boat decoy.

In the meantime, the other two Russian ships had stopped and were showing flag-signals ; we turned cautiously in their direction and stopped about 500 metres away from them. In response to our signal the captains of both vessels came on board bringing their ships' papers, which showed them to be trawlers escorted by an armed patrol. We kept the two Russians as prisoners and presented them with cigars, which they gratefully accepted.

The Commander ordered the dinghy out, with Lieutenant W—— and four volunteers to row across and blow up the ships. Needless to say, I was one of the party. We bent to our oars with a will and made as much noise as we liked, for we knew that we were safe enough under those watchful torpedo-tubes of ours. The sea was covered with floating timbers from the sunken boat. As we drew nearer we were a little surprised to hear no sound from either of the vessels, which were made fast to each other ; the officer, a torpedo-stoker, and myself went on board. The crews, a mere handful of men, were standing nervously about the decks. After a brief colloquy, our officer told the men to get into their boats and row ashore. Plainly delighted at their release, they hurriedly collected their belongings and tumbled into the boats. The explosive cartridges were soon adjusted and the valves opened ; with a crash and a roar the two vessels soon followed their leader to the bottom.

On our way back, about 100 metres from our own boat, we let ourselves in for an unexpected ducking, as comical in appearance as it was, in fact, dangerous. One of the bow oars caught a crab, and in the process he gave the man beside me a tremendous blow in the back which knocked him forward on to the officer who was steering. The latter tried to catch the man, but in a twinkling we all found ourselves in the water, while the boat drifted away. After a few moments of yelling, kicking, spluttering confusion, I managed to extricate myself and tried to swim, encumbered though I was by my heavy leather overalls; but something had got hold of me. I struggled like mad to free myself, but my right arm was held as in a vice. Finally I got the man's head above the surface and we both frantically trod water. But when I felt another grip on my left arm I gave up hope. For a few seconds that seemed an eternity we sank and sank, but at last we rose again, gasping. Someone grabbed at my overalls; I tried to push him away, but he would not let go; then, to my horror, I caught a glimpse of his anguished face and gripped him even closer. My senses were reeling; I thought of God and of my mother, and almost screamed aloud as I struggled to keep afloat. I was nearly done, when I felt myself suddenly hauled out of the water, and in a second was sitting astride the capsized jolly-boat. On either side of it my two comrades, unconscious and half drowned, clung to my leaden arms. I heard voices that seemed to come from very far away . . . and knew no more.

I awoke on our boat to a pleasant fragrance of hot rum, and next day all five of us, except for heavy colds in the head, were none the worse.

Then for home. One morning we fell in with a German mine-sweeping flotilla, escorted by five torpedo-boats and a small cruiser making at full speed for Kiel after a successful voyage.

Whether the U-Boat decoy that we had sunk had had time to send out wireless signals for help, or whether, by an accident not uncommon in the war, one warship had been steaming for hours quite unknowingly close behind another—in any case, several masts became visible on the horizon. We were soon able to recognise them as Russians making towards us—two cruisers escorted by two destroyers dashing zig-zag-wise to left and right. We dived at once, hoping for a chance of planting a torpedo into one of them. As we dived, I marked the great curved plumes of water at the bows of the racing destroyers—a lovely sight. Like maddened horses they dashed upon the enemy in despite of death. But there came no order to attack; the Commander decided to dive deeper, and at last we lay in utter silence at a depth of 40 to 50 metres. Soon we heard the thudding of propellers above our heads; then seven or eight dull explosions at different distances: depth-charges. Once again all was still. Slowly and cautiously we rose to the surface. The cruisers were making off. Any attempt to pursue them would have been imprudent owing to the ever-present danger of mines. So we hurried westwards at full speed.

We had now been nine days at sea. The appearance of a seaplane with blue, white, and red markings drove us under water for a couple of hours. Then we rose and proceeded on our course at full speed. Towards evening it grew very rough, and the look-out men were soaked to the skin when they came below. By morning, however, on the tenth day, the storm had blown itself out. Once more we were alone on the vast expanse of waters, plunging forward into the splendour of a glorious day. But about noon our cheerfulness was rudely shaken. A suspicious glittering something, like a highly polished jam-pot, emerged for an instant above the now peaceful waters and was gone.

" Diving-stations ! "

As we raced for the hatchways we saw a white streak hissing across the waves towards us ; a sharp turn of the helm to starboard, and the torpedo shot past us 5 metres off our bows. We dived, turned back on our course, and congratulated ourselves on our escape. What had my officer said when I was saying good-bye? " Helm hard a-starboard, and good luck." Kismet !

When the sun rose next morning above Swinemunde, we lay peacefully anchored off shore, much admired by summer visitors of all ages. We sat and sunned ourselves on deck, puffed at our cigars, and celebrated our safe return to the strains of a concertina. After one day's rest we put to sea again, and made our way unmolested into Kiel harbour, where the U-Boat Memorial stands to-day : an eagle with mighty outstretched wings, to the enduring glory of the countless dead heroes of the U-Boat Service, a monument of faith kept and still to keep.

25

SURRENDER OF A U-BOAT TO ENGLAND

By

Leading Seaman O. Wehner

DAYS, months, and years of glad and loyal service lay behind us. It was November 18th, 1918. A week before, we had been cruising off the Shetlands ; now we lay at anchor in Heligoland harbour ; to-morrow we were to put to sea and surrender our boat to the enemy. With bitterness in our hearts we thought of the last voyage that lay before us, as we spent our last hours in putting ashore our ammunition and all superfluous material.

Dawn broke on the 19th. A few hours earlier, the *Heligoland* had appeared off the harbour ; she was to escort the U-Boats to England and bring the crews back to Wilhelms-haven. About twenty U-Boats were there assembled, and at 8 a.m. we all cast off. Moving in a double line, we went out to meet the warship, which was lying about a mile to westward of the island. Two torpedo-boats followed us a little later. A funeral procession. All that day and the following night we kept a uniform speed of 8 knots an hour.

On November 20th, at 2 a.m., while it was still pitch dark, an array of floating lights appeared and overtook us ; it was our fleet : battle-cruisers, cruisers, and destroyers, steaming at 15 knots an hour to Scapa Flow. We could not take our eyes off these proud undefeated veterans of the sea. As they gradually disappeared northwards, tears came into our eyes, for we were sure we should never see them any more. We had lived through some stern and dreadful hours in the life-story of humanity, and in that moment we seemed to endure them once again.

The *Heligoland* anchored at 10 a.m., between the Dogger and Terschelling banks, just where our armoured cruiser *Blücher* was sunk in a glorious but unequal encounter in 1915. The U-Boats ahead of us—60, 62, 100, and 95—transferred their provisions, mess traps, and hammocks to the *Heligoland ;* we came slowly alongside in our turn and did likewise. About 1 p.m. we resumed our course at the same speed towards the English coast.

Night had long since fallen, and the fatal 20th drew near. About 1.30 a.m. we fell in with the hospital ship *Sierra Ventana,* the escort of the first U-Boat convoy, which was now conveying home the crews. Our feeling of weariness now lifted. We had reached the English mine-barrier, 30 miles distant from the coast. The English should have been here to meet us, but no doubt they had been delayed by the thick weather. From 7 to 8 o'clock we lay at anchor ; then an English light-ship became visible, and we steered towards it on a course of 230 degrees. Finally some seventeen clumsy-looking English destroyers made their appearance, and with them a small cruiser and a captive balloon. The English cruiser now took the lead, followed by the *Heligoland,* the destroyers steaming on either side of us. The time was past 10 a.m. The cruiser kept on signalling with her searchlights. More and more English ships came out to meet us as we drew in to the coast, which, though still 10 miles away, was quite visible, in spite of the haze ; Harwich was clearly to be seen. About this point the *Heligoland* stopped. We kept on our course, and ten minutes later cast anchor. A French airman circled over us once or twice, then an English destroyer came alongside.

English officers and men climbed down on to our deck. Then followed some minutes of silent and almost unendurable strain. Our hearts nearly ceased to beat, and we bit our lips in defiance of our shame. No, not shame, for we thought with pride of all our victories and heroic deeds, and with sorrow of our ruined Fatherland. When the English flag was hoisted we turned our backs on it, and looked towards our own land, and the future. Our Commander took a few English officers and engineers over the boat ; we stayed on deck forward, and the British sailors aft, so that they should not be contaminated by revolutionaries like us.

On we went once more, past several destroyers, on which we contemptuously turned our backs. On the mole and all the quays stood vast inquisitive crowds, and many films and photographs were taken. We entered the harbour and made our way past a swarm of war-vessels of all sizes. A number of small U-Boats, with all their crews on deck, lay on the port side of the mole. Finally we made fast to a buoy. A motor-boat came alongside, into which we stowed our remaining provisions. In spite of all we had gone through, it was with a heavy heart that we bade farewell to our U-Boat.

We were taken off by the destroyer F 64, and while aboard her were restricted to the deck amidships ; fore and aft, English sailors kept guard with machine-guns at the ready and deck-guns cleared for action. Fear tempered with respect ! However, one by one, they gradually came up to us ; and English sailors might have been heard asking for bread and jam, which seemed to indicate that they were very hungry. As we were pretty well off for supplies, we gave them some, receiving soap in exchange.

By way of impressing us, the English ships that came into contact with us had been freshly painted and supplied with new flags ; the decks of the destroyers were laid with coconut matting, and new uniforms had been issued to the crews.

At last the torturing hours of surrender were over and we began our voyage home. Once more we passed huge crowds of silent watchers ; once more we were filmed and photographed. By 4 p.m. we were alongside the *Heligoland ;* the other English destroyers and an armed trawler came up one by one, and 700 men gradually assembled on our cruiser's deck. It may here be mentioned that no sooner had the

English ships got 100 yards away than the coconut matting, etc., was hurriedly removed. Nothing but bluff; we had suspected it all along.

Shortly after 5 p.m. the *Heligoland* weighed anchor and steamed homewards at 17 knots ~~an hour~~. In the meantime we made ourselves comfortable in the gun-turret, and talked about the revolution, which, to us, was little more than a fairy tale; and one after another we fell asleep.

On the evening of the 22nd the outline of Heligoland came into view, and, soon after, we passed the island on our way to Wilhelmshaven.

The most terrible hours of a terrible four years were over. Never again should we have to face so shameful a voyage. Only an iron sense of duty sustained us to keep faith, for love of our people, even against our own conviction, and only the faith that we could help Germany in these hard hours, gave us strength for the ordeal. Our faith in the spirit of the German nation, that will guide it out of the pit of humiliation, enables us to look with steady eyes into the future.

EPILOGUE

By

Commander Karl Neureuther

SUCH are the voices that reach us from that heroic epoch which, as time hurries by, we are already beginning to forget, though they are but ten years gone.

These narratives are not written in the style of history. They are the very stuff of experience, unadorned ; and in them our gallant German sailors speak of what is most deeply imprinted on their memories. They come before the reader in this book, one after another, to tell it in their own words. They relate only what they themselves have seen and suffered. These stories must be taken just as they were told in the language of the tellers, unaltered in form and content. These simple narratives, therefore, whether they come from the fo'castle or the conning-tower, the engine-room or the stern torpedo-room, or wherever the narrator endured his hours of agony and peril, give and always will give, as a whole, the truest, most human, and indeed the best picture of that strange conflict—the German U-Boat war, so rich in victims and in victories, and withal so tragic.

What is the strongest general impression left upon us by these narratives ? Surely the deep and loyal conception of unity among a small group of men bound to each other by a common destiny, and all intent upon a mighty purpose. It was this community of labour, this absolute interdependence of aim, that fused all sections of a U-Boat crew into a whole. Not only the Commander was entrusted with the weal and woe of those under his command ; even the humblest seaman held in his hand the fate of the whole company. This fact is expressed by the U-Boat medal that, after three successful voyages, was awarded to every member of the crew without distinction, as significant of the fact that success was only made possible by the most intimate loyalty of deed and intention.

On all fronts, enemy as well as German, many heroic deeds were done ; but seldom can there have been so closely knit a body of men as that little company that faced their common

I had a friend."

fate within the narrow compass of a submarine.   Every one of them stood at the mercy of his fellows, and the perils that beset them are only too clearly revealed by the many U-Boats that were destroyed by the enemy.   No wonder, then, that the bonds that united such men have outlasted the years that followed the war.

From this fast fellowship comes to-day the joyful cry :

" And yet we live ! "

We live indeed, and in us there still lives what helped us to endure those dreadful perils—what carried us to victory and brought us home : our joy in deeds well done. We yet live :— we who fought beneath the sea ; and with us and near us live thousands who fought on other fronts—in the air, in the trenches, and beneath the earth ; and near us, too, stand those who fought against us. A strong inner life inspires us all and makes us one. We know the meaning of that moment when a man's life is as nothing ; we know those minutes when a man's existence hovers upon a thread of destiny, and its continuance is no more than a shining dubious " perhaps." We know what it is like when a man puts his life into the hands of his fellows, his superiors, or those under his command. But all these experiences must have come most deeply home to U-Boat sailors. They had to offer up themselves and the supremest efforts that a man can make—a little isolated band of men on a waste of waters far away from their homes, which often heard no more of them than the single word " Missing " or " Overdue."

We, fighters from many fronts, reflect on the great experience that unites us, on the times when we stood side by side, each man for all ; on those moments when we flung our own existence into the tremendous conflict. But this very experience taught us one thing which we must never forget— that men can and ought only to sacrifice themselves for what is worthy of that sacrifice.

Fighters we were, and fighters let us always be, but we will not fight the battles of avarice, aggression, and false prophets ; we will fight only for ideas that stand so high that they will summon back the great experiences of those great years. This stern resolve will be the noblest memorial to all those comrades, on whichever side they fought, who can no longer join us in the cry :

" And yet we live ! "

www.ingramcontent.com/pod-product-compliance
Lightning Source LLC
Chambersburg PA
CBHW030404100426
42812CB00028B/2831/J